THE SHARQI ARCHITECTURE OF JAUNPUR

ARCHAEOLOGICAL SURVEY OF INDIA

THE SHARQI ARCHITECTURE OF JAUNPUR;

WITH NOTES ON ZAFARABAD, SAHET-MAHET AND OTHER PLACES IN THE NORTH-WESTERN PROVINCES AND OUDH.

By

A. Fuhrer, Ph.D.,

OF THE ARCHAEOLOGICAL SURVEY, NORTH WESTERN PROVINCES AND OUDH

WITH DRAWINGS AND ARCHITECTURAL DESCRIPTIONS,

BY. ED. W. SMITH,

ARCHITECTURAL ASSISTANT

EDITED

BY JAS. BURGESS, LL.D., C.I.E.,

DIRECTOR-GENERAL OF THE ARCHAEOLOGICAL SURVEY OF INDIA

GYAN

Published by

GYAN

Gyan Publishing House
5, Ansari Road
Daryaganj, New Delhi-110002
Phone: 011-47034999, 9811692060
E-mail: books@gyanbooks.com

Distribution Network
gyanbooks.com
India, USA, Canada, UK, Australia, France

ISBN : 978-81-212-2740-7 (HB)
First Published, 1889

2nd Impression 2021

Printed at: Gyan Press, Delhi.

The Sharqi Architecture of Jaunpur
Author: A. Fuhrer

THE SHARQI ARCHITECTURE

OF

JAUNPUR;

WITH NOTES ON ZAFARABAD, SAHET-MAHET AND OTHER PLACES IN THE NORTH-WESTERN PROVINCES AND OUDH.

BY A. FÜHRER, PH.D.,
OF THE ARCHÆOLOGICAL SURVEY, NORTH-WESTERN PROVINCES AND OUDH.

WITH DRAWINGS AND ARCHITECTURAL DESCRIPTIONS,

BY ED. W. SMITH,
ARCHITECTURAL ASSISTANT.

EDITED

BY JAS. BURGESS, LL.D., C.I.E.,
DIRECTOR-GENERAL OF THE ARCHÆOLOGICAL SURVEY OF INDIA.

CALCUTTA:
PRINTED AND PUBLISHED BY THE SUPERINTENDENT OF GOVERNMENT PRINTING, INDIA.
CALCUTTA—THACKER, SPINK & CO. BOMBAY—THACKER & CO., LD.
LONDON—TRÜBNER & CO. AND W. H. ALLEN & CO.
1889.

Photo-etching. Survey of India Offices, Calcutta, December 1897.

PREFACE.

THIS volume is the first of the new series of Reports, begun after the re-organization of the Archæological Surveys in Upper India in 1885. In directing these surveys, my aim has been to have the Report volumes, as far as practicable, exhaustive and final on the subjects treated of in each. Much of course will be discovered everywhere in the future; but the monumental archæology can be fully dealt with, and a report—consisting chiefly of cursory notes on places visited on a flying tour, with rough drawings and photographs of the more notable buildings and sculptures met with, and speculations on matters on which the surveyor does not possess the materials for anything better than a mere hypothesis more curious than scientific—is not what ought to be considered satisfactory. Government has wisely forbidden the indulgence of the propensity to start such profitless speculations by the surveyors in their reports; and this volume will be found to be a plain statement of historical facts based on original sources of information relating to the places and buildings described, with careful and accurate representations of the monuments and their details sufficient to illustrate them—if not in every detail, yet quite as fully as is needed to give a complete idea of their architecture.

As Provincial Archæological Surveys had been conducted, at considerable expense, both in the Panjâb and North-Western Provinces, by officers of the Public Works Department, for several years previous to 1885, and as it had been devoted chiefly to the great monuments in Âgrâ, Jaunpûr, Dehlî, Lahôr, &c., I had hoped to be able to utilize and publish much of the material thus collected, and so make it accessible to the general public. On obtaining from Government a loan of these drawings, however, it was disappointing to find that, though numerous, technically well finished, and to large scales, the details—on which so much of the real character and style of architectural art is dependent—had not been measured and drawn with necessary care. Many of the smaller measurements were largely in error, and the proportions of ornamental work, mouldings, &c., overlooked. To have published such drawings would have been to produce untruthful impressions on the minds of such as should study them. Instead of the work at Jaunpur, therefore, being only to supply such additional details as had been overlooked in this extensive series of drawings, and write the desirable letter-press to accompany them, it was soon found that the whole must be re-measured and re-drawn, if the representations were to be accurate in all details. Mr. Ed. W. Smith, the Architectural Assistant, only joined the staff in February 1886, and without any qualified draftsman to assist him. In the short period available till the hot season set in, he completed the work on the Atala and Lâl Darwâza Masjids. Next cold weather he was engaged in Bundelkhand and elsewhere, and only returned to Jaunpûr in October 1887, when, with the native draftsmen he had been training, he made the drawings now published of the Jâmi Masjid. This Report had been prepared in October 1886 and went to the press in 1887, but the earlier plates had not been nearly all printed off when the later ones were received to complete the work.

The bulk of the letter-press is by Dr. Führer, whose trained and varied scholarship is a sufficient guarantee for its accuracy and research. The architectural descriptions of the buildings were prepared by Mr. Smith. My work has been to unite these into one connected account, to supervise the printing, and pass the drawings through the press. To the MS. of his report Dr. Führer added a bulky appendix of forty-six inscriptions collected during his tour between 14th February and 31st March 1886. These were in Arabic, Persian and Sanskrit, many of which were unknown before. 'Some of these inscriptions,' Dr. Führer mentions, 'are of great historical importance, especially in settling the question of the time of the first appropriation of the ancient Buddhist and Hindû temples by the Musalmâns.' The Arabic and Persian inscriptions, being mostly short, and belonging directly to the buildings described, have been engrossed in the text: the longer Sanskrit ones, as directed by Government, have been kept for separate publication in the *Epigraphia Indica.*

Besides the monograph on the Sharqî architecture of Jaunpûr, the report contains notes on the archæological remains at Zafarâbâd, Bhulla-Tâl, Ayodhyâ, and Saheṭ-Maheṭ, which places Dr. Führer visited in the course of his tour.

The plates have been reproduced by photo-lithographic processes at the Survey of India Office in Calcutta, but on account of other and more pressing demands,—to which these plates had often to give way,—the work has been much protracted. Nothing, however, could exceed the ready attention and interest bestowed from first to last upon it by Colonel Waterhouse, to whose care much of their excellence is due, and for which my best thanks are owing. They alone form a most important contribution to Indian monumental archæology, and will, apart from all description or comment, be found of much interest by the architect, the artist, and the historian of Indian architecture.

JAS. BURGESS.

CALCUTTA,
The 5th February 1889.

CONTENTS.

LIST OF PLATES.

REPORT

OF

THE ARCHÆOLOGICAL SURVEY OF INDIA.

JAUNPÛR.

CHAPTER I.

HISTORY.[1]

REGARDING the pre-historic ages, the consideration of legends and of the present distribution of clans will give matter for a theory as to the importance and direction of each wave of conquest which in succession swept the aborigines from the land. In the earliest times, the region round Jaunpûr was held by the Bhârs, an aboriginal race of whose civilisation we catch glimpses by no means according with our ideas as derived from the present condition of their outcast descendants. Along the banks of the Barṇâ are the sites of large cities, destroyed by fire, perhaps when Brâhmanism won its final victories over Buddhism; on the Gûmtî stood vast temples which perished on the first inroad of the Musalmân; but what founders and what antiquity these cities and temples boasted none can now say.

Yet a local legend gives a hint of one stage of the great conflict, when the aborigines were sinking but not yet wholly subdued. When the great Râmachandra ruled in Ayodhyâ, there dwelt in the curve of the Gûmtî, where now Jaunpûr stands, the giant-demon Karâlavîra (Karâr Bîr).[2] And whereas the highways were unsafe by reason of his violence, Râmachandra marched against him in person, and having vanquished him in single combat, left the giant's trunk lying as a memorial and warning, but flung his limbs and head to the corners of heaven. Over the trunk the demon's followers built a temple, paying divine honours to their lost lord. So far the legend; translating it, we suspect the truth to be that in some battle here the Bhâr hero fell before the might of the invader, and the honour his sorrowing clansmen paid to his remains in time so

[1] Sources: Faqîr Khair-ad-dîn Muhammad 'Allâhâbâdî's *Jaunpûrnâmah*, ed. Jaunpûr; *Târîkh-i-Firishta* of Muhammad Qâsim Hindû Shâh Firishta; *Târîkh-i-Mubârak-Shâhî* of Yahyâ-bin-'Ahmad-bin-'Abdullah Sîhrindî; *Târîkh-i-Fîrûz-Shâhî* of Ziâ-ad-dîn Barnî.

[2] Fîrûz Shâh found here a temple dedicated to Karâlavîra (Karâr Bîr) within the lands of mauzâ Karâr. The Hindûs named the new fort Karâlakoṭa (Karârkoṭ), and the ground adjoining to the north is still known as mahallâ Karâr. An equally probable interpretation of the myth is that Karâr is the name, not of a single hero, but of a class of Bhârs. Karârkoṭ, the eastern pargaṇa of Jaunpûr, may be supposed to derive its name from the same class. Under the southern wall of the fort still exists the shrine of Karâlavîra, partly covered by the stones of the fallen wall, but still the scene of worship. The object worshipped is a large stone, bearing a rude resemblance to the upper part of a human trunk, smeared thickly with turmeric, &c., so that it is impossible to say what kind of stone it is.

impressed his enemies that they in time, assigning a different origin to it, joined in the same worship

Then for ages we have not even the light of a myth. Mr. Ommaney[1] found in Bandelkhand an inscription,[2] which spoke of a Yavanapura on the Gûmtî, and this he identified with Jaunpûr. In this, however, he was certainly wrong, for there can have been no town of any size here when Sâlâr Masa'ûd Ghâzî destroyed the temples of that ancient town, to which, three centuries later, was given the new name of Zafarâbâd; but as the ancient name (Ratagaṛh) of the fort only of this city has been preserved, the inscription may refer to it. The Yavanendrapura of the *Harivaṁśa* may be taken as referring to the ancient town that existed on the site of the present Zafarâbâd, though General Cunningham's reading of "Yamonyâpura," in an inscription on a pillar in the west cloister of the Lâl Darwâza masjid at Jaunpûr,[3] must be rejected. Buddhism seems to have been strong here, for the temples remaining even to the Musalmân period were undoubtedly Buddhist, and of sufficient magnificence not only to furnish materials for the conqueror's masjids, but to supply models even for the details of their decoration. For miles in the southern corner of the district, between the Basohî and Barṇâ brooks, are found the sites of cities destroyed by fire, of whose former grandeur the peasant will tell, though now but scant traces are left of them but those Buddhists in character. But as the dawn of our present history draws on, we find the country subject to the Pâla princes of Banâras as in mythic times it seems to have been to those of Ayodhyâ, and with Banâras it finally fell under the sceptre of the Musalmân, when Muhammad Shahâb-ad-dîn Ghorî defeated Jayachandra II. in A.D. 1194. Not that Shahâb-ad-dîn was probably the first general of Islâm who had triumphed so far to the eastward. Of the terrible Mahmûd of Ghaznî, indeed, no march is recorded farther east than Kâlañjara, and we may be sure that had he taken Banâras history would not have been silent, and Shahâb-ad-dîn's four thousand camel-loads of spoil would have been the vaunt of an earlier triumph. But the fame of such a city cannot but have reached the great iconoclast's ears, and nothing is more probable than that he would send forth such a force as he could spare to lay waste the lands of idolaters. Hence we yield credence to the tale of the writers of the *Mirât-al-Asrár* and *Tawáríkh Munimí*, that Sâlâr Masa'ûd Ghâzî, sister's son to Mahmûd, starting from Kanauj, overran much of the country north of the Ganges, carrying his ravages to the gates of Banâras and destroying the temples of Zafarâbâd before meeting his death, in the prime of youth, in battle with the Hindûs at Bahrâich. But we are travelling beyond the record. Sâlâr Masa'ûd Ghâzî is a personage little more historical than Râmachandra himself, and the temples of Zafarâbâd may have been among the thousand Shahâb-ad-dîn boasted he had overthrown. But whatever the date of their destruction, it is probably the same as that of the first foundation of Jaunpûr.

The prince, who dwelt in Ratagaṛh, sickened with the desolation round his walls, built for himself a palace and temples a few miles to the west, on a spot somewhat more secluded on the north bank of the Gûmtî and near the old temple of Karâlavîra. In the two centuries and a half which elapsed between the conquest by Shahâb-ad-dîn and the

[1] *Gazetteer of the North-Western Provinces*, Vol. XIV, Part III, page 83.

[2] This inscription has never been published, and the original cannot now be found.

[3] Published by Cunningham, *Archæological Survey Reports*, Vol. XI, page 126. I read this as "Ayodhyâpura" at which the grandfather of Padmasâdhu had lived.—J. B.

accession of Fîrûz Shâh, many fine buildings had risen in the new city, untroubled by wars or by the Musalmân occupants of the mother-city, which by degrees passed wholly into the hands of the invaders. In the reign of 'Alâ-ad-dîn Muhammad Shâh, in 1300 A.D., one Shaikh Bârha converted the only temple[1] former ravagers had spared into a masjid, still standing; and, but a few years later, died, and here was buried the local "light of Hindûstân," Sadr-ad-dîn Chirâgh-i-Hind, whose tomb, still standing, was built by Zafar Khân, the new founder of Zafarâbâd, and apparently the first governor of Jaunpûr. As there was frequent intercourse between the court of Dehlî and the semi-independent princes of Lakhnautî, and as the main road, crossing the Ganges at some ford not far west of the present city of Farrukhâbâd, ran through Zafarâbâd and Banâras, many armed and many peaceful parties of Musalmâns had visited the place between the plundering foray of Shahâb-ad-dîn and that long halt of Fîrûz when the present city of Jaunpûr was founded. Indeed, this was perhaps not the first visit even of Fîrûz, for when, in 1355, he marched against Hâjî Iliâs of Lakhnautî, who had entered his kingdom westward even to the gates of Banâras, he probably passed at least on his homeward march through Zafarâbâd.

But in A.D. 1359[2] Fîrûz was moving against the successor of his old rival, and was overtaken by the rains at Zafarâbâd, and halted there till autumn. He despatched an embassy to the prince, against whom he was marching, but, though the envoy sent brought rich presents in return, among which are mentioned five elephants,—an offering which the custom of those and later times seems to have considered a confession of inferiority,—the weather only delayed the king's march. In the camp was Prince Fath Khân, then a child of seven, that eldest and most beloved son whose death fifteen years later, A.H. 776 (A.D. 1374), plunged Fîrûz into uncontrollable grief and the empire into severe troubles. At this time the father was thinking much of his son's training, and though, in the next season's march, his fondness conferred on the child the ensigns of royalty, his care at the same time appointed proper tutors for his education.

The idea of founding a city in the neighbourhood, which might form a proper basis for future campaigns, was probably conceived at that time; for, though his march was

[1] Fergusson seems convinced that nowhere have the Musalmâns appropriated a Buddhist building without reconstruction, and he is probably right; but, when treating of the Atala masjid, he only gives as his reason for his thinking it reconstructed, that certain conspicuous parts are undoubtedly Saracenic. But at Zafarâbâd there are no such parts. The roof is flat, and the interior is a hall, 18 feet high, 9 bays deep, from east to west, and 7 broad, from north to south. The outer ranges of columns are double, and plain walls close the spaces between the outmost. The square pillars are somewhat irregularly placed towards the western sides; the aisle, running from the door to the *qibla*, is 8 feet 6 inches broad, the others 6 feet 6 inches, the greater breadth of this centre aisle is certainly suggestive of Musalmân interference in its construction; and the arch which once finished the front is most probably a part of the original design. The real date of Shaikh Bârha's interference cannot be fixed with accuracy; the stone on which the dedication was carved fell from the front and is lost, but the inscription is said to have given a verse from which certain words were picked to give the date A.H. 711 = A.D. 1311, but 'Alâ-ad-dîn Mahmûd Khiljî is said to have been named as the then ruler, and his accession dates half a century later. Sharaf Jahângir, a foreign saint who died here in the autumn of 1397, had lodged in this masjid. The Zafar Khân mentioned was probably Zafar Khân Fârsî, who, coming from Sunârgâon in Bengal ten years before that inroad in which Jaunpûr was founded, was made Nâib Vazîr, and twenty years later Vazîr; he betrayed his master and disappears suddenly. But Firishta names several others and gets confused among them.

[2] Though there can be no real doubt as to the chronology, it is not wholly undisputed. Khair-ad-dîn first speaks vaguely, but as assuming the place to have been founded by Fîrûz about A.H. 760 = A.D. 1358; in another place he gives the date plainly as A.H. 772 = 1370, but says it is recorded by *abjad* in the words *Shahr Jaunpûr*, which gave the year 770. Firishta speaks of the halt at Zafarâbâd on the eastward march in 760, and at "Zafarâbâd and Jaunpûr" on the return in 761; the *Jahânârâ* says that Fîrûz founded the city on the eastward march, Khair-ad-dîn and the *Târîkh-i-Muhammadî* (the latter giving the date A.H. 775 = 1373) on his return. Jayachandra II. seems to have been dispossessed of Ratagarh in 1359: so the claims of the two years 1359 and 1360 are pretty equally balanced. The plan may have been adopted in the former, and carried out in the latter.

almost unopposed, and Sikandar Shâh lost no time in making terms, Fîrûz, marching back to Zafarâbâd, deliberately halted for another season. Leaving the wide-spread ruins of the old city, he found, at a little distance to the west, but on the other bank of the Gûmtî, a thriving town, built by those who had left their old homes and brought their gods to a more sheltered spot. This city he determined to enlarge and name after himself, and though some dream, it is said, made his predecessor, Malik Jûna, who had reigned as Muhammad-bin-Tughlak, the epodonymic hero of Jaunpûr, Fîrûz did not change his other plans of giving to the new city all that could make it pleasant and famous.

One morning, in April 1360, Fîrûz rode over from Zafarâbâd, attended by Jayachandra, a Râjpût prince of the Gaharwâr clan who seems to have been at that time dispossessed of Ratagaṛh, and compelled to take up his residence in his father's palace in Jaunpûr. At the end of his journey he found a thriving town extending for some miles along the northern bank of the Gûmtî, and boasting four large temples, two at least conspicuous both for size and costliness, a palace, and a tank of cut stone, the main body of which was a quarter of a mile square. The two chief temples first attracted the king's notice, but, though the people looked on and worked patiently while he threw down the temple of Karâlavîra, cast up a mound on its site, and built on it and round it a fort with stones brought from the ruined temples of Zafarâbâd, an attempt to desecrate the temple of Ataladevî met with so fierce a resistance that, after much bloodshed, Fîrûz was compelled to make a compromise and give a written undertaking that the temples should be left untouched and Hindû worship tolerated, stipulating only that the temple of Ataladevî be left unrestored and perhaps unused. The return of the cold season brought other labours to Fîrûz, and appointing Zafar Khân to the charge of the frontier provinces, he left the city Jaunpûr for the first and last time. Still, we are told, he bore his new city in fond remembrance, and took care to settle in it men both of learning and wealth. But few particulars can be recorded; Zafar Khân is remembered solely as having, in this very year, built the tomb of the local saint, a plain Pathân dargâh with short pillars supporting a square dome; and if we add that when, in 1376, governors were appointed to divers provinces, "Jaunpûr and Zafarâbâd" fell to Malik Bahrûz, we have told all that concerns Jaunpûr before died Fîrûz, her founder, on the 23rd October 1388,—a prince who, with Sher Shâh, her most famous *alumnus*, contests with Akbar, the founder of the city whose growth was her destruction, the glory of being the greatest prince on the roll of Indian kings.

The short and troubled reigns which fill the space between the death of Fîrûz and the accession of Mahmûd Tughlak on the 5th April 1394, contain nothing to interest the historian of Jaunpûr, except the tale of the gradual rise of Khwâja Jahân, the first independent prince of Jaunpûr. This noble, by name Malik Sarwar, was a eunuch, given by Sâlâr Rajab to his grandson Muhammad. In the household of this prince he rose to be Khwâja Sarâ (chief eunuch) and controller of the elephant stables, and following his master's fortunes through all troubles, on his temporary success in A.D. 1389 was rewarded with the title of Khwâja Jahân and the office of Vazîr. In the following year, the ability of a rival having given Muhammad a stronger hold on the throne, the prince rewarded his new supporter with Khwâja Jahân's office; but on the fall of the new Vazîr in the course of the next year, Khwâja Jahân, on whose head his rival's blood is thought to rest, regained his office, and retained it till he was sent by Maûmûd Tughlak, in March 1394, with the title of "Malik-as-Sharq," to govern the frontier provinces of the East. Years before, his notice had been attracted by the childish beauty of Malik Vazil, the son of Qaranfal,[1] a slave and water-bearer of Fîrûz; and having adopted him, he took him, now in the prime of life, with all his brothers, to his new government.

The charge of the Malik-as-Sharq was far more important, as his title was higher than that of the former governors. Malik Bahrûz had "Jaunpûr and Zafarâbâd," with such provinces to the eastward as were held neither by petty chiefs nor the lords of Lakhnautî; to this were added the lower Doâb and the provinces on the left bank of the Ganges, which previously had been assigned to other hands. There was no question as to the success of his administration. Forts which had fallen into the hands of the Hindûs, provinces which had revolted, again owned the supremacy of Dehlî, and Khwâja Jahân, amid his peaceful labours in Vijayachandra's palace in Jaunpûr, was perpetually cheered by news of the triumphs of his adopted son—triumphs the fruits of which he fully enjoyed when—Tîmûr having driven the Tughlaks from Dehlî—he felt able to proclaim his independence and rule with undisputed sovereignty over the rich provinces which lie between the Himâlayan Tarâî and the Jamnâ, from Kol and Rahîrî to Tirhût and Bihâr. It cannot, of course, be said that his authority was so powerful in the half-conquered Gorakhpûr or the remote Tirhût as at his palace gates in Jaunpûr. The power of a native prince varies inversely as the distance from which it is exercised, and the Hindû Râîs, who from the huge fort of Etâwa looked down on the ravines of the Jamnâ, may well have been like the Perceys of the Scottish marches. Yet when the kings of Lakhnautî who faced Fîrûz and had exchanged embassies and made treaties with the kings of Dehlî, paid the tribute due to Dehlî to the new prince at Jaunpûr, we may be sure that his titles "Sulṭân-as-Sharq Atabûk Azîm" were no empty vaunts, and that his successor found the sceptre he had helped to raise no mere reed. Khwâja-i-Jahân had made his adopted son his deputy with the title Malik-as-Sharq, and he again had given the command of the fort and the city to his brother Ibrâhîm. Whether or not the heir was present in Jaunpûr in the former half of 1400, when Khwâja Jahân died, or was absent on another such expedition as that which, in the spring of 1396, had made the princes of Bengal pay tribute, his interests were well looked after, and his succession was undisputed. But the stupor of exhaustion which had followed Tîmûr's departure from Dehlî was by this time passing away, and Mallû Iqbâl Khân, who was ruling Dehlî under cover of Mahmûd Tughlak's name, felt strong enough to resent the boldness of the new prince in assuming the regal canopy, coining money, and being publicly prayed for as Mubârak Shâh Sharqî. But first, in the winter of 1400-01, Mallû Iqbâl subdued Shams Khân of Bîânâ and levied contributions in Katehar, and afterwards, apparently late in the hot season (1401), marched from Dehlî, supported by the forces of Shams Khân and Mubârak Mewâtî, against Mubârak. At Patîâlî the allies were vainly opposed by the Râî of Mâînpûrî, but Mubârak seems not to have

[1] Firishta and Abûl Fazl agree that Qaranfal was the name of the child, not of his father. There is perhaps no good reason for following the *Târîkh-i-Muhammad*, as we have done in the text; but the author of the last-named work gives details instead of letting the adopted son appear only when the throne was vacant. It is worth while to mention here that, in the very few lines Abûl Fazl gives to the reign of Ibrâhîm, he mentions the defeat and punishment of the rebellion of Qaranfal, possibly the father of Ibrâhîm and so nearer of kin to the former prince.

crossed the Ganges and to have borne the loss of Kanauj without resistance. The swollen river was probably the cause of his patience, and the same obstacle kept the two armies facing one another on opposite banks for two months, neither daring or being able to force a passage, till want of supplies compelled both to retreat. But Mahmûd Tughlak at this time returning from Gujarât, Mallû Iqbâl resolved to try whether the presence of the emperor would do more than his name, and Mubârak, taking up his old position on the left bank of the Ganges, died here in the autumn of the same year while waiting for his enemy to appear.

The vacant throne was at once filled by Mubârak's younger brother Ibrâhîm, with the title of Shams-ad-dîn Ibrâhîm Shâh Sharqî, a prince of varied talents, whose long reign is the most glorious in the short annals of Jaunpûr. As soon as the great news of his brother's death reached him, he hurried to the army on the Ganges where an event soon occurred which tried all his skill in kingcraft. Mahmûd Tughlak had showed no ability in the years before Tîmûr's invasion, when he was, at least in name, supreme, and his hurried flight to the court and contemptuous hospitality of the governor of Gujarât had not raised his reputation. When weary of his retirement, he returned to Dehlî, at the invitation, or by the permission, of Iqbâl Khân, to be the puppet and prisoner of a man ruling in his name; and when now brought face to face with the army of Jaunpûr, to try whether the magic of his name and ancestry would shake its allegiance and make easy his tyrant's victory, he conceived the vain hope that, were he once within the lines of the enemy, the new prince might abdicate in his favour or at all events free him from his bondage to Iqbâl. But, though Ibrâhîm was young both in years and in power, he was far too able to be a pawn in any man's game; and when Mahmûd took advantage of a hunting party to escape from Iqbâl's hands, he was received with great reserve by the Sharqî prince, being even, according to some writers, denied fire and water. Covered with disgrace, he returned to the Dehlî army, but was suffered to take possession of Kanauj and administer it himself; the more readily, no doubt, that it was debatable ground,—for even when wresting it from Mubârak, Iqbâl had been compelled to leave the government to the person appointed by Mubârak's predecessor. Leaving Mahmûd in quiet possession, the two armies moved to their respective headquarters, and so ended the first war between Dehlî and Jaunpûr.

Iqbâl Khân fell on the 18th November 1405 in an attack made in conjunction with Bahrâm Khân, another governor and guardian slave of Fîrûz, on Khizr Khân, Tîmûr's deputy in the Panjâb; and the officers left in command at Dehlî invited Mahmûd to return. He went with a small retinue to take possession, but speedily returned to Kanauj. In the autumn of the following year, Ibrâhîm marched to recover the place, and the armies took up their accustomed stations on the opposite banks, but after long halting and slight skirmishing, Ibrâhîm marched back to Jaunpûr. The slothful Mahmûd too presently retired to Dehlî, much to the disgust of his army, which either deserted him or was disbanded. As soon as this news reached his rival, he again put his army in motion, took Kanauj after a siege of four months, and having halted there for the rainy season of 1407, and then being joined by many of Mahmûd's nobles, made inroads on the territories of Dehlî. Of Baran he made Malik Marhabâ Khân governor, and Tâtâr Khân of Sambhal, but when he had already reached the banks of the Jamnâ and was about to attack Dehlî itself, he heard that Muzaffar Shâh (Zafar

Khân) of Gujarât, having subdued Hûshang Shâh of Mâlwâ, was marching to attack Jaunpûr. To secure his capital, therefore, he retreated, and straightway (April 1408) Mahmûd captured Baran by assault, killing Ibrâhîm's governor, drove Tâtâr Khân of Sambhal to Kanauj and appointed Asad Khân governor of Sambhal on his own part. Kanauj remained the frontier town of Jaunpûr till the death of Mahmûd in February 1412 ended the line of Fîrûz.

After the death of Mahmûd, Ibrâhîm formed the idea of making himself master of Dehlî, and made a few marches thitherwards, but speedily returning enjoyed near fifteen years of unbroken peace. His court was a haven of rest for the many learned men driven from the favoured places by the endless contests of the times, and their fame and the noble buildings which still adorn his capital are the enduring glories of his reign. The masjid, pavilions and baths of the Fort are memorials of his boyish employment as his brother's deputy, but the great Atala masjid was finished and dedicated in December 1408, and about the same time probably those which his nobles built on the sides of the two other great temples named and spared by Fîrûz. To this long rest too may probably be assigned the plan of building a bridge opposite his palace, an idea which none of his successors worked out, and of a second large masjid the building of which was the glory of Husain's reign, as its dedication was the consolation of his fall. As famous in this time, though nearly forgotten now, were the doctors of his court, to whom doubtless was chiefly due that fame for learning which Jaunpûr has hardly yet lost, though, through the decay of native learning and the waning prosperity of the town, the so partly endowed schools which existed even in Muhammad Shâh's reign have left few traces. Foremost among them and founder of the most famous school was Qâzî Shahâb-ad-dîn Malik-al-alâmâ, "one of the most renowned names," says Abûl Fazl, "for wisdom and learning." Driven from Dehlî with his master Mullâna Khojahgî, by the irruption of Tîmûr, he was honourably received by Ibrâhîm, who loaded him with honours, and to whom he dedicated several works, the *Sharh-i-Hindî* and the *Irshâd-al-Nahwâ*. A rival of the philosopher was the holy Shaikh Badî-al-Hakkwa-ad-dîn Shâh Madâr who died in January of 1438—four years before his successful rival, and was laid in a great tomb built for him by Ibrâhîm at Makanpûr,—his general dwelling-place between Kânhpûr and Farrukhâbâd.

The march of Ibrâhîm towards Dehlî, in the winter of 1413, had been provoked by the vain desire of Daulat Khân, who for a time filled the throne of Dehlî after Mahmûd's death, to compel Ibrâhîm to raise the siege of Kâlpî, and the speedy counter-march was probably caused by news that Khizr Khân, with his northern levies, had compelled Daulat Khân, after a siege of three months, to abdicate, and had settled himself quietly in the vacant throne. Although the Sa'îd princes were feudal superiors rather than despots like the Moghals and levied their revenue rather by forays, and as reliefs, than by organized taxation, their power was steadily growing, and Ibrâhîm did not care to force matters to extremity when opposed to Sa'îd Mubârak in A.H. 831 (A.D. 1427).

In that year he was marching against Kâlpî, when there suddenly appeared in his camp Muhammad Khân, the rebel prince of Biânâ, who, leaving his fort with Sa'îd Mubârak's forces before its walls, had hurried to get help from Ibrâhîm. Aroused by expresses from Kâdir Khân, the vassal ruler of Kâlpî, and doubtless also warned of the movement of Muhammad Khân, Sa'îd Mubârak marched in person against Ibrâhîm.

The division which Ibrâhim had detached, under his brother Mukhlis Khân,[1] to reduce Etâwa, was driven back by a force sent from Atrolî; but when the two armies marched in parallel lines from Atrolî and Burhânâbâd, Ibrâhîm reached the Jamnâ at a point west of Etâwa, and so must have been able to make himself master of that important fort. On the banks of the Jamnâ, and but a few miles apart, the two armies lay facing each other for three weeks, till weary of indecisive skirmishes, on the 21st March the Sharqî prince offered battle. The challenge was accepted, and from noon, till darkness separated the combatants, the battle raged with fury. Both armies lay on the field that night, but the next day, possibly after negotiating a hollow peace, and sealing it by a royal marriage of Mubârak's daughter Bîbî Râjî to the heir of Jaunpûr, Ibrâhîm returned to Jaunpûr.

Another expedition against Kâlpî was the last active operation of Ibrâhîm's reign. In the autumn of 1435, he and Hûshang of Mâlwâ formed, apparently much at the same time, the plan of occupying Kâlpî; but when the two armies were facing each other near the place, and a battle was hourly expected, news reached Ibrâhîm that Sa'îd Mubârak too had heard of his march from Jaunpûr and was preparing to attack that city. Unwilling to face the forces of the two kingdoms at once, Ibrâhîm retreated and left Hûshang to make himself master of Kâlpî. His two rivals died in no long time, but Ibrâhîm never again attempted Kâlpî, spending the few years left him at home, and dying in the winter of 1440 full of years and honours. "He was an active and good prince," says Abûl Fazl, "equally beloved in life, as he was regretted by all his subjects." Able, liberal, a bigoted Musalmân, and a steady, if not a bloody persecutor, he was a successful ruler and a patron of learning; and though we may agree with Akbar that his dynasty might have built more bridges and fewer masjids, we are certainly not disposed to blame the munificence which erected the Atala masjid.

Mahmûd, eldest son of Ibrâhîm, succeeded without opposition, and reigned as prosperously as his father for nearly twenty years. Two years after, in 1442, complaining to the king of Mâlwâ that his vassal of Kâlpî was neglectful of the laws of Islâm, he obtained permission to attack that place; but when he had seized and plundered it, he was less attentive to the remonstrances of the suzerain who was much busied in other quarters. The king of Mâlwâ then moving to restore his vassal, in A.H. 818 or A.D. 1444, the armies met and skirmished near Îrish; but an attack on Jaunpûr itself being threatened, Mahmûd agreed to a peace, negotiated by a doctor of high repute (variously recorded as Shaikh Jamâl-ad-dîn Sadda and Shaikh Jânîda) whereby Kâlpî and its neighbourhood was, after a short delay, restored to Nâsir, son and successor of Kâdir the former ruler. The forces thus set free, Mahmûd employed in extending his power in other quarters, first reducing Chunâr and its neighbourhood, afterwards apparently the last possession of his house, and then laying waste and plundering Orissa in a holy war.

Before narrating the events of that attack on Dehlî which was Mahmûd's first movement after a six years' rest, it is necessary to narrate briefly the rise of the new antagonist and future conqueror of Jaunpûr. The eventful action between Khizr Khân and the Tughlak was determined in favour of the former by the valour of Malik

[1] Malik Khâlis and Malik Mukhlis are named by other authors as nobles of Jaunpûr in high office and as *chelas* of Fîrûz; they, too, were the builders of the plainest, and probably the oldest, of the masjids in the Jaunpûr style; there seems little risk in identifying Malik Mukhlis with the general Mukhlis Khân.

Sulṭân, an Afghân chief who slew Malik Iqbâl with his own hand. The gratitude of Khizr Khân changed the name of his champion to Islâm Khân, and conferring on him an important government, he gave him opportunities of providing for his many brothers. On his father's death in battle, Bahlol joined his uncle Islâm Khan with whom he obtained such distinction as to be wedded to his cousin, adopted, and to the exclusion of legitimate sons, declared his uncle's heir; and after considerable opposition, even Quṭb Khân, Islâm Khân's son, made his submission, and by his constant fidelity was the chief support of Bahlol's power. Profiting by the growing weakness of Sa'îd Muhammad, Bahlol, Ibrâhîm Shâh Sharqî and Mahmûd Khiljî of Mâlwâ annexed more and more of the Dehlî territory; but when, in the year of Ibrâhîm's death, the Khiljî marched to the gates of Dehlî, Sa'îd Muhammad implored Bahlol's help, and though in spite of a treaty concluded between the two emperors, Bahlol plundered the retreating Khiljî, Sa'îd Muhammad could not punish his disobedience, but was compelled publicly to adopt him as his son. On the accession of Alâ-ad-dîn, Bahlol abstained from taking the oath of allegiance, but followed the imperial standard in an attack on Bîânâ in A.H. 850 (1446), whence the weak emperor retreated in haste on the mere rumour of the Sharqî prince's planning a march on Dehlî. The fancy Alâ-ad-dîn now took for the retirement of Badâun favoured Bahlol's designs on Dehlî, and, accordingly, after two attacks he captured and established himself in that city, A.H. 854, with the full consent of Alâ-ad-dîn, who, by reason of the adoption of Sa'îd Muhammad, regarded Bahlol as a brother, and only asked to be left quiet in Badâun. Two years later, in the spring of 1452, when Bâyazîd was in command at Dehlî, his father Bahlol being absent warring in the Panjâb, Mahmûd Shâh Sharqî, aided by Daryâ Khân Lodî, governor of Sambhal, laid siege to Dehlî, but the hurried return of Bahlol from the northward and the questionable fidelity of Daryâ Khân made the invader plan a retreat. This, however, was delayed so long that something like a pitched battle occurred between the forces of Bahlol and a strong division of Mahmûd's army under Faṭh Khân, a native of Hirât. An elephant belonging to the latter being wounded by an arrow of Quṭb Khân, then apparently, as often afterwards, commanding for his cousin Bahlol, the line was broken, and Quṭb Khân, finding opportunity to reproach Daryâ Khân, the latter deserted his new allegiance, and Mahmûd's forces were utterly defeated with the loss of seven war elephants, much baggage, and of Faṭh Khân. Again a few years of peace occurred till A.H. 861; in the winter of 1456-57, Bahlol marched against Etâwa, and Mahmûd at the instigation of Jûna Khân, who had been made governor of Shamsâbâd on deserting Bahlol, hastened to oppose him. After lying face to face for a short time, the princes made terms and respectively retreated; the country was to be divided as in Sa'îd Mubârak's time, Faṭh Khân's elephants were to be given up, and Jûna Khân expelled from the territories of Jaunpûr. But after the treaty was concluded and both armies had marched away, Bahlol became too impatient to wait till the autumn should make him peacefully master of Shamsâbâd, and surprised and occupied it; and Mahmûd, hurrying back in wrath, was taken ill and died in his camp near that place on the very morning after a night attack on his camp, wherein Quṭb Khân, cousin and brother-in-law of Bahlol and commandant of the attacking column, was taken prisoner.

The only remaining work of the reign of Mahmûd Shâh Sharqî is the masjid called Lâl Darwâza, built by Bîbî Râjî, his queen, as a dependency of her palace without the walls and endowed as a school. Of the palace, from whose "high gate painted with vermilion," the present name of the masjid is derived, no trace is left: it was destroyed by Sikandar Lodî in his rage at the ingratitude of Husain. This same Bîbî Râjî, who was a daughter of Sa'îd Mubârak of Dehlî, seems to have been a woman of energy and ability, and in the short reign of her son are found many proofs of her influence; for, to begin with, though Firishta speaks of Bhîkun Khân, Mahmûd's successor under the name of Muhammad, as the eldest son of the deceased, allusions by the chronicler Faqîr Khair-ad-dîn seem to show that his right to the throne was questioned. Still he was in camp with his father, and Bîbî Râjî managed to seat him on the throne, and then negotiated a treaty with Bahlol, who had drawn up his army in battle array before news of Mahmûd's death reached him, in the same terms as that of the preceding summer. The two princes then marched homeward, Muhammad Shâh with his prisoner Quṭb Khân, to disgust all at Jaunpûr by his cruelty and irritable temper, from which the dowager queen was the heaviest sufferer, and Bahlol to find the gates of Dehlî shut in his face, and to receive a message from Shams Khatûn, his wife, that, if he meant to sit at home while her brother was a captive, he had better sit in the *zanâna* while she led his army. Stung by this scornful message, he retraced his steps, but Muhammad Shâh had been so much more rapid in his movements that Bahlol found Râî Karan, his governor, expelled from Shamsâbâd and his enemy Jûna Khân reinstalled by Muhammad Shâh. In camp with the Sharqî prince were his younger brothers Husain and Jalâl; but Hasan, the elder and his rival, had stayed behind in Jaunpûr and sorely troubled the king's mind with fear of treachery. In vain were orders sent that both the prince Hasan and the prisoner Quṭb Khân should be put to death; the Kotwâl replied that Bîbî Râjî guarded them too carefully; and so, by inviting his mother to camp to consult about an appanage for Hasan, Muhammad cleared the way for his jealousy and his own fall. Before Bîbî Râjî had arrived at Kanauj, news of her son's murder reached her; and while she stayed mourning at that city, the other sons took alarm, and Husain succeeded to get despatched with a strong force to intercept a pretended attack of Bahlol. Before Bahlol's forces Husain retreated quietly to Kanauj to be received with open arms by his mother. Jalâl Khân attempting to join Husain was captured by Bahlol. Muhammad Shâh, alarmed at these defections, also retreated on Kanauj, to find that Husain had assumed the ensigns of royalty, and had all his army drawn up to oppose his brother. Deserted by all his officers, the unfortunate Muhammad Shâh had to flee, but the same valour which had made Pratâp Singh of Mâinpurî think it safer to face Bahlol than Muhammad Shâh, would have made him a dangerous foe, but that Bîbî Râjî bribed his armour-bearer to break off the points of his arrows, so that he fell by treachery in an orchard after a short reign of five months.

After punishing those officers who had seemed unfavourable to his cause, Husain marched against Bahlol; but a truce for four years, ratified by the exchange of Quṭb Khân for prince Jalâl, was agreed on, each party keeping its own possessions; and to this truce we may probably assign that marriage of Husain to Bîbî Khonza,[1] daughter of 'Alâ-ad-dîn, ex-king of Dehlî and still king of Badâun, which had consequences so

[1] Other writers give the name of Husain's consort as Malika Jahân and make her the daughter of Sa'îd Mubârak and so aunt of 'Alâ-ad-dîn. She was a very firebrand, always pining for the magnificence of Dehlî, known to her only by hearsay, and dangling before her husband's eyes the glory of being sole lord of Hindûstân.

fatal for the eastern kingdom. The four years' truce gave time for an expedition to Orissa which greatly increased Husain's wealth and fame. Mubârak Khân of Burhânâbâd, fearing the influence with Bahlol of his rival Daryâ Khân, long governor of Sambhal, and one of the most powerful vassals of Dehlî, took refuge with Husain. The vassal princes of the central Doâb, always wavering, were so far favourable to Husain as to throw no obstacles in his way, when—after exacting tribute from the Râî of Gwâliâr in the winter of 1470-71—he advanced on Dehlî. Bahlol hurried back from the Panjâb, and leaving Dehlî in the charge of his faithful cousin, met Husain's army on the Jamnâ not far east of Âgrâ. After a week's skirmishing a three years' truce was made; and at the end of that time Husain besieged and took the fort of Etâwa, and gaining over the border vassals marched on Dehlî, but after some indecisive skirmishes made a new truce and retired, only to indulge himself in the same amusement a few months later.

The last-named futile expedition must have taken place about the end of 1474 and was the last which left Jaunpûr still a worthy rival of Dehlî; for the short peace which now ensued was the last. In the autumn of 1477 Bîbî Râjî died at Etâwa, and Quṭb Khân of Râprî, coming with the râjâ of Gwâliâr on a visit of condolence, by way of making his court to Husain, spoke disparagingly of Bahlol and volunteered to support his host's claims to Dehlî; but, having taken leave, he hurried to Dehlî with stories of Husain's designs and his own recent flight. From that moment both sides prepared for war. In the summer of next year the ex-king Alâ-ad-dîn died at Badâun, and Husain, after performing the funeral ceremonies, also seized the territory to the prejudice of his brother-in-law. Marching thence he occupied Sambhal, imprisoning Mubârak Khân, who had returned to his former allegiance and succeeded his rival Daryâ Khân in the government of that province, and marched on Dehlî. Again Bahlol hurried back from Sirhind, and after Husain had had the better in several skirmishes, a treaty was negotiated through Quṭb Khân, Bahlol's cousin, whereby the upper Doâb was assigned to Bahlol, but all lands east of the Ganges to Husain. But as the latter was marching homewards, Bahlol attacked his rear, killed great numbers of his men, captured many officers of rank with some treasure and equipage, and occupied the parganas from Kol to Shamsâbâd. Husain promptly gave battle, and after an indecisive combat a peace was again patched up, Dupamau being made the common boundary. Husain could not forgive Bahlol's perfidy and again waged war, but now with continued ill success. Defeated in an obstinate battle with the loss of his baggage, he retired on Râprî; driven thence, he moved to Gwâliâr, and having been anew furnished with money and stores by the râjâ, he marched on Kâlpî. Meantime Bahlol compelled Husain's brother Ibrâhîm to surrender Etâwa, and moved to meet his enemy at Kâlpî. After some time he discovered a ford, crossed the Jamnâ and defeated Husain, and—after one last battle near Kanauj—Husain had to flee on foot to Badâun, pursued as far as Haldî,—even his seraglio falling into the hands of the victor. After recruiting his army, Bahlol advanced without further check to Jaunpûr, so that the kingdom fell in the same year which had seen it attain its greatest extent.

Although the advances Bahlol had made on different occasions,—professing his attachment to the dignity he had supplanted, with which Husain was connected by marriage if not by descent, or asking only to let alone,—were probably such artifices as he had found successful in gaining him the throne, he was no ungenerous victor. He allowed Husain to reside at Jaunpûr and finish the great masjid (*masjid-i-jâmi*) and to retain possession of a tract of country, probably round Chunâr, yielding five lakhs[1] a year. Having appointed Mubârak Khân Lohânî governor of Jaunpûr and stationed his faithful cousin Quṭb Khân at Bisaulî, near Badâun, as governor-general and commander-in-chief, Bahlol halted for a time at Badâun. The value of Quṭb Khân's fidelity was now strikingly manifested, for on his death at this time his many friends prepared for revolt. Among them was Mubârak Khân, and Husain vainly hoped in the confusion to recover his old kingdom; but Bahlol without delay marched to Jaunpûr, made his eldest surviving son, Bârbak, viceroy and drove Husain away, yet still charged Bârbak not to interfere with him in his estates. In no long time the growing infirmities of his great age made Bahlol anxious finally to settle his affairs. Declaring Nizâm his successor and conferring on him the government of Dehlî and the upper Doâb, he took pains to secure his favourite from the hostility of his grandson Azîm Humâyûn and his son Bârbak, governor of Jaunpûr, separating their governments by others assigned to his most trusted officers, and soon after died in camp in the central Doâb in the summer of 1489.

By following the advice of Qatlagh Khân, the ex-Vazîr of Husain, Nizâm having escaped the dangers which threatened him personally, ascended the throne under the name of Sikandar, and after subduing nearer and less dangerous rivals, marched against Bârbak, who formally refused to do homage or to read Sikandar's name in the public prayers. The governor of Bahrâich, cousin to the two rivals, commanded a division of Bârbak's army, but being taken in the beginning of the first battle and received in a flattering manner by Sikandar, changed sides with the usual facility of the time, and charging his old friends, made all fear treachery and flee. Bârbak's valour could not restore the day, and he fled westward while his son was taken prisoner; but on his surrender, he was reinstated in his government of Jaunpûr as a check on Husain, who was still in force in Bihâr. But Bârbak was too weak for his work, and in the spring of 1492, Sikandar had scarcely reached Dehlî after a long and successful campaign, when he received news of a dangerous revolt in the old kingdom of Jaunpûr. Bârbak had fled to Bahrâich, Mubârak Khân of Karrâ had been taken prisoner, and his brother, who also held a government of some importance, killed. But the march of Sikandar soon caused the release of Mubârak Khân and the return of Bârbak; and the rebels having been defeated at Katgar, Bârbak was reinstalled. But even the near neighbourhood of the emperor could not insure Bârbak's good conduct or make his subjects bear his tyranny; for in less than a month, while Sikandar was still marching about, there was another outbreak when Bârbak was committed to safe custody and his government entrusted to Jamâl Khân, the first patron of Sher Shâh. In the winter of the same year the emperor made a reconnaissance of Chunâr—still in the possession of Husain; but, though he repulsed a sally of the garrison, he doubted his power to capture so strong a place and marched along the right bank of the Ganges, receiving on his way the submission of the Gaharwâr râjâ of Kantit. In the winter of 1494-95 he again marched to the south and east, but—being overtaken by the rains—after losing from natural causes most of his cavalry, fell back on Jaunpûr for supplies. Hereupon Narsingh Râî of Kantit sent word to Husain in Bihâr of the crippled state of his enemy; but Sikandar had no

[1] The *Mirât-al-'Âlam* says five karors of dâms, equivalent to twelve and a half lakhs of rupees.

sooner heard of Husain's movement than he hurried to meet him and defeated him in a great battle some two marches from Banâras on the right bank of the Ganges. Husain fled to the court of Gaur, was there courteously received, and died here in obscurity just five years later, but was buried in Jaunpûr. With him ended the Sharqî dynasty of Jaunpûr, of which the following is the chronology:—

A.H. A.D.

796 or 1394. Kwâjah-i-Jahân.

802, 1399. Mubârak Shâh, adopted son.

803, 1400. Shams-ad-dîn Ibrâhîm Shâh Sharqî, younger brother.

844, 1440. Mahmûd Shâh, son; associated his son in 861, died 863.

861, 1456. Muhammad Shâh, son.

863, 1458. Husain Shâh, brother, subdued by Bahlol in 879 or 881; fled to Bengal in 893 (?) and died in 905; his coins run on to 909.

892, 1486. Bârbak Shâh-ibn-Bahlol of Dehlî, appointed governor; removed in 899.

Having subdued Bihâr and exacted tribute from the râjâ of Tirhût, Sikandar returned to Jaunpûr, determined to leave no sign or trace that the hated family of Husain had ever existed. The great palace on the banks of the Gûmtî, that of Bîbî Râjî without the walls, the dower-house, and the burial-place under the shadow of the great Jâmi masjid, were all razed to the ground, and the utmost influence of the doctors of the law could scarcely save the masjids from utter destruction. The nobles of the court were encouraged to use these palaces as quarries, and the prolonged stay of Sikandar, who seems to have made this place his headquarters till after the death of Husain, was as little favourable to the place as the notion of his son Jalâl, the new governor, that it was less healthy than another site which took his fancy some eight miles to the north-east, on the right bank of the Sâî, where he and his nobles built palaces of which no trace is left, and the first of the three fine bridges which are still glories of Jaunpûr.

Sikandar died on the 14th December 1517, and the arrogance of his eldest son and successor Ibrâhîm soon so disgusted his nobles that they conspired against him with Jalâl. The latter was at Kâlpî, which was also under his charge, but he had not reached Jaunpûr, where he was to be enthroned, when the conspirators changed their minds and determined to stand by Ibrâhîm. But Jalâl thought himself too far committed, and though his friends fell off from him daily, he placed his family in safety at Kâlpî and marched on Âgrâ. Here the governor amused him with negotiations till Kâlpî had fallen and Ibrâhîm in person was at hand. Jalâl then fled to Gwâliâr, but after divers escapes was captured and murdered. His government of Jaunpûr was entrusted to Daryâ Khân Lohânî, who died shortly after Bâbar's invasion. His son and successor Bahâdur was chosen leader and under the title Sulṭân Muhammad proclaimed king by the Afghâns after Ibrâhîm's defeat and the capture of Âgrâ,—and so for a short time again Jaunpûr was the capital of a kingdom which extended from Oudh to Bihâr. But when Humâyûn, dry-nursed by Fîrûz and Mahmûd Khân, both old servants of the Lodî house, led the chief part of the Moghal army against the confederates, the latter slowly retired first on Jaunpûr, then on Bihâr, and by the end of 1525 Jaunpûr had for ever ceased to be independent. Humâyûn spent his short stay in Jaunpûr in endeavours to renew its prosperity and ancient glories, even restoring in some part, with the old materials, the buildings which had been quarries for Jalâl's new palaces at

Jalâlpûr; and when recalled to command in the great war of the next spring, he appointed Junaid Birlâs governor with his own two advisers and Qâzî Abd-al-Jubbâr as a sort of council of regency. Three years later Bâbar himself must have visited the place when on his march against Mahmûd Khân, king of Bihâr, but afterwards repulsing that prince he contented himself with a charge to Junaid to continue the war in conjunction with Jalâl,[1] ex-king of Jaunpûr, and returning to Âgrâ died there on the 24th December 1530.

As the great and successful rival of Humâyûn was connected by many ties with Jaunpûr, it is necessary briefly to sketch his rise. He was the eldest legitimate son of Hasan Khân, an Afghân favourite of Jamâl Khân, the successor of Bârbak in the government of Jaunpûr. But Hasan so neglected his wife and her sons that Farîd, leaving his father's house at Sahsarâm, took service under Jamâl Khân, refusing to return home on the pretence that at the capital he had more opportunities for acquiring learning: and he is said greatly to have profited by these opportunities. When three years later Hasan came to Jaunpûr, Farîd was reconciled to his father, who, wishing to live at Jaunpûr, made over charge of the jâgîr to his son. The father afterwards promised to make Sulaimân, a younger son by a concubine, his heir; but on Hasan's death Farîd obtained the patent from the king, and Sulaimân took refuge with Muhammad

[1] This Jalâl-ad-dîn Nasrat Shâh Sharqî, ex-king of Jaunpûr, is about as puzzling a personage as it is easy to find; and but for the necessity of speaking of the pretended descendants of the ancient princes who still dwell at Jaunpûr, one would have been tempted to leave out all mention of one who really plays so small a part. He prepared a "royal entertainment at Karrâ" for Bâbar on his eastward march in the winter of 1528-29 and "was honoured with an audience." He can therefore hardly be that son of Bahlol who was so mature at his father's death forty years before as already to be governor of Kâlpî; besides no connection of that prince with Jaunpûr is recorded. Nor can he be Jalâl, the son of Sikandar, who did assume the title of king of Jaunpûr; for it is distinctly recorded that he was put to death by his brother Ibrâhîm; and even though he had escaped and had somehow acquired estates and government in his old appanage of Kâlpî, he would not have marched in Bâbar's train against his brother and clansmen in Bihâr. If we could account for his presence in Karrâ, we should say that this ex-king was probably Jalâl Khân, son of the Afghân pretender Muhammad Shâh Lohânî, set up at Jaunpûr after Bâbar's defeat of Ibrâhîm Lodî; when driven out of Jaunpûr the same family ruled in Bihâr, and shortly before the present march, Sher Shâh had supplanted this prince, his former pupil, and driven him to Bengal. But we have not yet exhausted the subject, for Khair-ad-dîn, who takes more interest in *minutiæ*, does not, with Firishta, record the Sharqî dynasty as extinct in Husain, but gives him a son, Jalâl-ad-dîn, married to the only child of Nasîb Shâh, king of Gaur, whom he succeeded—apparently in Husain's life-time, for he sent Husain's corpse to Jaunpûr. Now Husain certainly is buried at Jaunpûr, and though Sikandar was more employed in the west in the later years of his reign, yet turbulent as his nobles were, large bribes must have been offered before any governor of Jaunpûr would have let his master's special enemy be solemnly laid in his ancestral tomb, in the house Sikandar had with such pains destroyed; a more probable solution would be that at some later time, possibly when the Afghâns were strengthening their hands against Bâbar, Husain's bones were exhumed and re-interred. But at all to fit in Khair-ad-dîn's genealogy with Firishta's, it is necessary to rely much on possible changes of name; Nasîb Shâh must be identified with 'Alâ-ad-dîn Husain Shâh, the king of Gaur, with whom Husain took refuge, who reigned from 1498 to 1521 and who was succeeded successively by his sons Nasrat Shâh and Mahmûd, and these must be supposed to prove adoptions by his son-in-law Jalâl and his grandson. Scarce credible as this may seem, Jaunpûr was the chief part of the bribe said by Khair-ad-dîn to have been offered by Humâyûn to Mahmûd Shâh of Gaur as the price of his support against Sher Shâh; from Firishta one would rather think that Mahmûd would have been as much surprised as pleased by his ally's help to recover possession of his late kingdom of Gaur. Khair-ad-dîn adds that Mahmûd fell in the great battle near Kanauj, 1540, wherein Sher Shâh overthrew Humâyûn, but was supported in his last moments by his generous enemy who laid him with his fathers in Jaunpûr and enriched and protected his family. The heir of the dead man, then a child, was known as Sultân Husain, *alias* 'Umar Khân; he used his wealth to restore in part the dower-house and to decorate and improve the capital of his ancestors. His descendants retained more or less of dignity, but Khair-ad-dîn gets confused about them about the time of 'Alâmgîr. There is no doubt that the present occupants of the old house are representatives of Mahmûd Shâh Pûrbî. The steps by which the Sharqî dynasty became blended with the Pûrbî are less clear.

The house so often called the dower-house is separated only by a lane from the northern cloister of the Jâmi Masjid. Sikandar broke down to the level of the court all the buildings but the cloister in the grave-yard; 'Umar Khân's repairs made habitable part of the adjoining court. The basement was left uninjured; to this as to other buildings older edifices furnished materials; it is an oblong of some one hundred and ninety feet by one hundred and forty, having at all corners the foundations of round turrets.

Shâh Sûr, a distant relative, governor of the district—not the province—of Jaunpûr. This noble, failing in an attempt to make Farîd share the administration as well as the property with his brother, became his bitter enemy, and was planning his ruin when Bâbar's invasion threw everything into confusion. Farîd at once joined the Afghân pretender, who was set up at Jaunpûr, was made tutor of his son Jalâl, and on an act of conspicuous valour was honoured with the title of Sher Khân. But his old enemy managed to change the Afghân prince's mind against Sher Khân, who was at last compelled to take refuge with Junaid Birlâs, already governing Karrâ, and with his help he recovered his old jâgîr together with other districts, all of which he held of the Moghals. But he had no foolish prejudices for loyalty, and finding an opportunity, returned to nominal allegiance to Muhammad Shâh Lohânî, now ruling only Bihâr, whose son and successor Jalâl he soon after supplanted, partly in self-defence. But when Mahmûd Lodî, son of Sikandar Shâh, fled before Humâyûn from Chitor to Patna, and was there chosen king of Bihâr by the Afghân chiefs, Sher Khân had to submit, obtaining only his old jâgîr and a written promise that on recovery of Jaunpûr, Mahmûd would yield Bihâr to his vassal ally. Hereupon forces marched against the Moghals, who evacuated the whole province of Jaunpûr. Humâyûn was engaged in the siege of Kâlañjar, but advanced to the support of his deputy. Sher Khân thought himself slighted in the distribution of commands in the Afghân army, and wrote to Amîr Hindû Beg, who had probably already governed the city of Jaunpûr, promising not to oppose the Moghal, and his defection in the battle of the next day was the chief cause of the defeat of the Afghâns. But, not long after Junaid Birlâs had been re-installed at Jaunpûr, Humâyûn sent Amîr Hindû Beg to demand of Sher Khân the surrender of Chunâr, and though more urgent affairs distracted his attention while Sher Khân's power was growing, yet the sudden outbreak of the Afghâns, on the death of Junaid Birlâs, compelled Humâyûn to march to Jaunpûr in the summer of 1536, and his success there and in Bengal was the proximate cause of his ruin; for, while he was loitering in the east, his brother Hindâl Mîrzâ revolted; and after his terrible defeat near Baksar in 1539, Humâyûn quite lost for the time his hold on Eastern India. Jaunpûr indeed held out for a short time under Amîr Hindû Beg and his son Bâbâ Beg Jalayûn, but before his great victory on the 17th May 1540, Sher Shâh was undisputed sovereign of all India east of Âgrâ, and 'Âdil Khân, his son, was his viceroy in Jaunpûr.

In the troubles which preceded the return of Humâyûn, Jaunpûr with the other eastern provinces changed masters a dozen times; but its fort was no longer the chief place of strength, for the possessor of Chunâr—fortified as a treasure-house by Sher Shâh—was of necessity supreme. Nor does it play any conspicuous part in the early part of Akbar's reign, at least till the rebellion of Alî Qulî Khân, Khân Zamân. This noble, an ally of Bairâm Khân, had been made governor of Sambhal by Humâyûn, and in the year 1558 he was made also governor of Jaunpûr and *Panjhazârî*. In no long time he expelled the Afghân governors from the adjoining districts, and when—three years later—the Afghâns of Bengal attempted to recover the frontier provinces, he and his brother Bahâdur Khân utterly defeated them. Yet this success nearly resulted in Khân Zamân's ruin at court, for he withheld the customary offering till Akbar had led a strong army as far eastwards as Karrâ. The clemency which left this insolence unpunished was but ill requited, for in 1563 began the troubles with Alî Qulî Khân which only ended with his death in battle on the 6th June 1567, and the execution of some of his Uzbak allies, who were taken at the same time and trampled to death by elephants at Jaunpûr—almost as part of the ceremonial which attended the installation of Khân Khânân Munim Khân in that rich and important government. During these years Akbar's headquarters seem to have been alternately at Jaunpûr and Chunâr, and the province may not have been formally entrusted to any one till Munim Khân received it after Khân Zamân's death; for more than once it was restored to the traitor on his pretended and temporary submission. But any detail of the operations seems to pertain rather to general history than to the special history of Jaunpûr.

One event, however, must be noted:—when the mother of Khân Zamân was confined in the fort of Jaunpûr under the charge of Ushraf Khân the governor, her brother's son, Bahâdur Khân, in the summer of 1536, with a stronger force surprised the fort, burnt the gates, broke down its chambers, imprisoned the governor, rescued his mother, and after plundering the city, returned on Banâras, and when he heard of Akbar's advance, breaking down two arches of the Jalâlpur bridge to prevent pursuit. It is scarcely credible that even after this revolt Khân Zamân was re-installed in his government, and that not till he was actually killed did Akbar finally appoint his successor, conferring the government on Khân Khânân Munim Khân, the last viceroy who resided in Jaunpûr. For eight years after his death a new city and fort were built at the confluence of Ganges and Jamnâ, to be the headquarters of the viceroy of the East; and though the province of Jaunpûr was conferred on Khân Khânân 'Abdûr Rahîm in 1590, in lieu of Gujarât, he never seems to have visited his government, though he made or found his grandson, Ma'sûm Khân, *Nazîm;* and from that time the great of men of Jaunpûr was either the *Nazîm* or else the governor of the fort, who drew pay for himself and the garrison from certain small dependent parganas, and whose post was so little valued that in 1598 Jamâl Khân was about to break into open rebellion when invited to yield for this the government of the stronger fort of Chunâr.

CHAPTER II.

THE GREAT BRIDGE AND LATER HISTORY.

To Munim Khân Jaunpûr owes its most useful, if not its most beautiful, building, the great bridge. Yet if we here follow Khair-ad-din, whose narrative contains much local detail and is supported by the metrical dates inscribed on the piers, we find that Firishta's information is faulty in a period when naturally it should be best, for Khair-ad-dîn makes Munim Khân governor in A.H. 972 (1564) and in that year to have founded the bridge. As the following six inscriptions, Nos. I to VI, show, it was begun in A.H. 972 (1564) and finished in 976 (1568).

Inscription No. I is in Persian on the top of the third kiosk, on the right hand, north end of the bridge; lines 1 and 2 facing the south and lines 3 and 4 facing the north. Each stone is of greyish sandstone and measures 3′ 4″ by 8″; the characters are beautifully cut. The metre is *Hazaj* :—

مقامی ساخت سلطان السلاطین　　سرشته آب و خاکش از مسرت

بعشرت کامران بادا که آمد　　در او قبلهٔ ارباب حاجت

الهي! تاقیامت باد معمور　　ازین باني بنای دین و دولت

چو از پیر خرد تاریخ آن جست　　چنین پیر خرد گفتا بعشرت

1. The emperor built this place whose materials are impregnated with happiness.
2. May (*he*) ever live successful, for its door is the *qibla* of expectants!
3. O God! the foundation of religion and wealth may ever remain by its founder!
4. When (*I*) enquired the date from the old wisdom, the old wisdom replied "with pleasure."

The *abjad* powers of the letters for "with pleasure" give the date A.H. 972 (1564). Khair-ad-dîn mentions that "a poet found the date of its foundation in the words for 'with pleasure.' Khân Khânân therefore rewarded him with 972 gold mohars." The inscription itself is not given in the *Jaunpûrnâmah*.

Inscription No. II[1] is written in a mixture of Arabic and Persian prose on the top of the east wall, on the south end of the bridge, in seven lines, on reddish sandstone, each block measuring 2′ 10″ by 1′ 2″. The characters are well preserved.

این عمارت عالي و اساس متعالي در ایام

دولت حضرت العظم السلطان و الخاقان

مظهر المعظم آثار السلطان ظل الله

[1] Inscriptions Nos. II-VI were first published by the late Dr. Blochmann in the *Proceedings of the Asiatic Society of Bengal* for July 1873. Some of his readings are, however, incorrect, probably owing to the deficiencies of the rubbings supplied to him by General A. Cunningham. Faqîr Khair-ad-dîn in his *Jaunpûrnâmah* has only given inscriptions Nos. III and V.

ابو الغازي جلال الدين محمد اکبر بادشاه

از خالص مال صاحب خیری سمت اتمام

یافت که نام نامي و سال بنا و اتمامش

این کلامست چه باني این منعم خان

"This magnificent building and splendid foundation was successfully completed at the private cost of the bounteous Sire, in the reign of the great king, emperor, high representative of the emblem of royalty, shadow of God, the great conqueror **Jalâl-ad-dîn Muhammad Akbar Bâdshâh.**" The famous name and the year of foundation and completion is given in these words: "Its builder (*is*) Munim Khân." [A.H. 975 = 1567.]

In this inscription Akbar is called **Abûl Ghâzî** instead of **Abûl Faṭh.**

Inscription No. III is written in Persian verse on the top of the second pier, north end, on the west side, in six lines, on a reddish sandstone, measuring 2′ 10″ by 1′ 2″. The metre is *Mutaqârib-i-sâlim.*

زهی خان خانان منعم که باشد

درش قبله جمله دلهای آگاه

پلی بست از سنگ بر روی دریا

کزو بگذرد اهل دل گاه بیگاه

چو از فضل الله شد بسته این پل

ازان گشت تاریخ آن فضل الله

٩٧٦

1. The **Khân Khânân** of heavenly bounty,
2. Whose gate is the *qibla* (*Makka*) of all wise men,
3. Built a stone bridge across the river,
4. So that people may cross from time to time.
5. As this bridge is built by the grace of God,
6. Hence its date is *Fazli allah* ["grace of God"]. [A.H. 976 = 1568 A.D.]

Inscription No. IV is written in Persian prose on the top of the second pier, north end, east side, in four lines, on a greyish sandstone, measuring 2′ 10″ by 1′ 2″.

این پل باحکام عالی نتیجه مشایخ العظام

غوث الانام خواجه شیخ نظامي نظام الدین

پسر حضرت اعظم مخدومي شیخ عبدالعزیز

بهنرمندي نادر العصر استاد افضل علي کابلي باتمام رسید

"This lofty bridge was completed under the superintendence of the great Shaikh, just to men, **Khwâja Shaikh Nizâm-i-Nizâm-ad-dîn**, son of **Hazrat Makhdûm-i-'Abdul 'Azîz**, and under the guidance of the unparalleled architect (*ustâd*) **Afzal Alî Kâbulî.**"

Inscription No. V is written in Persian on the top of the first pier, north end, east side, in ten lines, on a reddish sandstone, measuring 3′ 6″ by 1′ 4″. The first eight lines are written in verse, the metre being *Ramal*, the last two lines are in prose. The characters are well preserved.

خان خانان خان منعم اقتدار

بست این پل را بتوفیق کریم

نام آن منعم ازان آمد که هست

بر خلایق هم کریم و هم رحیم

از صراط مستقیمش ظاهر است

شاه راهي سوی جنات النعیم

ره بتاریخش بري گر افگني

لفظ بد را از صراط المستقیم

۹۷۵

حق سبحانه تعالی باني این بنارا در پناه خود دارد

ناظم و کاتبه میر محمد محسن الدین اثیم است

1. **Khân Khânân Munim Khân**, the generous,
2. Built this bridge by the grace of God.
3. He is named **Munim** ["*one who confers benefits*"], because
4. He is gracious and merciful to the people.
5. His *Sirât-al-mustaqîm* leads the thoroughfare
6. Towards the gardens of heaven.
7. You will find its date if you deduct
8. The word "*bad*" from "*Sirât-al-mustaqîm.*"[1]
9. May the Holy God ever keep the founder of this building in His protection!
10. The composer and writer of these verses is **Mîr Muhammad Muhsin-ad-dîn**, a sinful man.

The value of the letters of the words "*Sirât-al-mustaqîm*" is 981, and if we subtract the value of the letters of "*bad*," i.e., 6, we get 981—6 = 975 A.H. = 1567 A.D.

Inscription No. VI is written in Persian verse, the metre being *Mujhas*, on the top of the first pier, north end, west side, in four lines, on a reddish sandstone, measuring 2′ 10″ by 1′ 2″. The characters of the first two lines have become partially obliterated.

این پل که به بست × × × × ×

× × × × × × بعرصهٔ تنگ چنان

تاریخ بنای آن چو جستم از غیب

گفتند پل محمد منعم خان

۹۷۵

[1] The faithful Musalmân before entering paradise has to pass over a bridge called *Sirât-al-mustaqîm*, "the established path," which leads over a bottomless abyss, but the path is as narrow and as sharp as the edge of a sword.

1. The bridge which has been built . . . .
2. . . . . in such a short time.
3. When I enquired from the invisible being the date of its foundation,
4. (*The angels*) said: "the bridge of Muhammad Munim Khân." [A.H. 975 = 1567 A.D.]

General Cunningham, in his *Archæological Reports*, volume XI, page 122, is quite in error in saying that "inscriptions in verse were placed on *every* pier giving the date and the name of the builder." There is no trace to be found of any inscription on the other piers, and all those extant are well preserved with the exception of No. VI.

It is curious that the great bridge should have owed its foundation to the humanity of Akbar and not to the munificence of Husain, who throughout his reign was contented to use a bridge of boats for his gorgeous processions to the *îdgâh* he had built on the south bank. For Akbar, who was very fond of boating, during his excursions saw one night a poor widow lamenting loudly that she could not get ferried across, and the emperor having taken her over, stationed boats at the ghâṭ for like purposes for the future, but also remarked to Munim Khân on the advantages of building a bridge there, somewhat disparaging the former kings for their preference of masjids. Further reference was made to the subject in next day's darbâr, and Munim Khân came forth from the presence, pledged, both in his own opinion and the emperor's, to build a great bridge in the place of the evening's adventure. The true bridge measures some 330 feet within the inner faces of the abutments, but as each pier averages 14 feet in thickness, the entire waterway is less than 200 feet. Of the ten arches the middle group of four are of perceptibly larger span than the three arches at each end, and the kiosks which—as is usual with Indian bridges—were added as decorations, adorn the northern middle arch. The bridge was built by a Kâbulî architect of the name of 'Afzal 'Alî at the expense of Munim Khân.[1] Khair-ad-dîn in his *Jaunpûrnâmah* states that "the builder is Fahîm Khân, governor of the fort and manager under Munim Khân and who appointed as his deputy Khwâja Dost, an Afghân Jâgîrdâr of Ghîswa who brought the chief masons from his own estates." But from history we know that Fahîm Khân was a slave of Munim Khân's successor, Mîrzâ Abdûr Rahîm; and Khwâja Dost is Khwâja Shaikh Nizâm-i Nizâm-ad-dîn of inscription No. IV. Of course the real cost cannot be even approximately guessed: it is said to have reached 30 lakhs,[2] but a vague expression makes one suspect that this round sum—if one could believe it to be anything more than a rough guess—included all moneys laid out on the Fort and other buildings; anyhow Khwâja Shaikh Nizâm took the credit to himself of saving materials enough to build a bridge and a mansion where the road to Ghîswa and Allâhâbâd crosses the River Sâî.

[1] See Inscription No. IV above.

[2] Another account makes the cost fourteen lakhs, an estimate which does not contradict the suggestions of the text that the thirty lakhs included the whole cost of public work. Of course, the whole is said to have been paid by Munim Khân. The bridge Pul Guzâr, about eight miles west of Jaunpûr, said to have been built from the leavings of the great bridge and finished A.H. 979 (A.D. 1569), carries the Allahâbâd road over the Sâî, at a height of twenty-five feet above the winter water-level, and the embankment of approach extends a long way on each side. Originally it consisted of eight 18-feet arches with piers of somewhat greater breadth; one or two arches had more than once been destroyed by floods and repaired; but when a pier was again broken down in the rains of 1847, arrangements were made for remodelling the whole. Two arches were in each case thrown into one, to the increased beauty of the bridge and improvement in every way. Another bridge of nine pointed arches, built in 1510 by Jalâl, son of Sikandar Lodî, ten and a half miles south-east from Jaunpûr, carries the Banâras road over the Sâî at Jalâlpûr.

On the roadway at the north end of the bridge, there is a large stone statue of a lion standing over a small elephant. The attitude is stiff, and the workmanship, especially of the legs, is hard, wiry, and unnatural. From the style of the sculpture it is clear that it must originally have occupied the top of some large gateway of one of the Hindû temples destroyed by Ibrâhîm or by one of his successors.

The bridge was not, however, the only work of Munim Khân. He built, besides several masjids, a palace for the governor in a walled garden adjoining the bridge on the northern bank; an outer gate of stone, adorned with coloured tiles, and an outer court for the fort; with several hot baths in different parts of the city which he endowed also,—that the citizens might use them without charge. For a general view of the great bridge see the frontispiece, Plate I.

Jaunpûr: Later History.

The connected history of Jaunpûr ceases with the foundation of Allâhâbâd; thenceforward it only appears at intervals like any other country town, and nothing further remains but rambling mention of different incidents in its steady decay. Aurangzîb visited the place, and but for court intrigues would have restored at all events the masjids to their former beauty. Near relations of 'Ahmad Khân Bangash lived here, and one of the first acts of his administration was to confer the government on them; that they ever succeeded in wresting it from the Nawâb Vazîr of Oudh is not so clear, though Sâhib Zamân Khân laid the country waste and partly destroyed the fort. Both Abûl Mansûr Khân and Sa'âdat 'Alî made long halts here, occupying the old palace of Munim Khân; but when the *firmân* of the four Sarkârs was conferred on Bâlwant Singh, the fort was still retained by the Nawâbs, and his little garrison repaired so much of the palace as was wanted for their own occupation.

When, however, this district passed into the hands of the English, though Chunâr was garrisoned, the fort of Jaunpûr was left to Chait Singh. Warren Hastings may have visited the city, Sir Eyre Coote certainly did, while Duncan's visit in 1788 is recorded in those volumes of *Proceedings* which are mouldering unnoticed on the record shelves of the Commissioner and Collector of Banâras. He writes too favourably of the site, and laments the decay of the town, telling how that once it was "the seat and resort of Muhammadan science and the residence of many of their learned men, insomuch that it was known by the appellation of the Shirâz of India." And with this tribute to the past fame of the city at the hand of the distinguished man who was the first European personally concerned in the administration of the city or province, the history of Jaunpûr may here close.

Vague as is our knowledge of the revenues of the kingdom of Jaunpûr, we have not material even for a guess as to the expenditure. Vast sums doubtless were lavished on jewels and shows after the usual fashion of native courts; wars waged by armies even of feudal militia are costly; yet if we go beyond such generalities we can only repeat tales of the schools founded, or run through the roll of noble buildings built by the kings of Jaunpûr. And though no trace be now left of these schools but the story of their past fame, we have better ground than Mr. Duncan's for saying that this city was the Shirâz or the mediæval Paris of India. Fîrûz determined to make it a seat of learning worthy of his cousin's fame. Each of the princes of Jaunpûr prided himself on patronising science, and the troubles which in the early part of the fourteenth century scattered the doctors of the ancient imperial city, were eminently favourable to the rise of a school of learning in the peaceful and secure Jaunpûr. Shahâb-ad-dîn and his master in Ibrâhîm's time, and the dozen holy men—who must have been more than mad beggars, if we may judge by the respect and attention they received from that able prince,—these were the first professors of Jaunpûr. Nearly at the same time with Bâbâ Nânak flourished Sa'îd Muhammad Jaunpûrî, founder of the Mahdî sect which—teaching severe asceticism and justifying its members in preventing breaches of sacred law even by slaying the offender—had to be put down with a little sharp persecution by Salîm Shâh Sûr. So great was the influence of Shâh Quṭb-ad-dîn, a blind devotee of Husain's time, that he was able to depute a disciple to act for him as Qâzî in Bhadohî. Even in Muhammad Shâh's time twenty famous schools existed in Jaunpûr of which now but the names are known, the founder of one having died in the middle of the fifteenth century, of another in the middle of the seventeenth. Nor was scholastic learning only cultivated: Husain is described as "a clever and luxurious prince, skilled in music, a connoisseur and a composer," and verses set to music of his composition are said still to exist. Sher Shâh did not want to study only the commentaries of Muhammadan doctors or the tenets of Sa'îd Muhammad when he refused to leave Jaunpûr for his father's hall at Sahsarâm. Of the successful cultivation of other arts let the noble masjids of Ibrâhîm and Husain bear witness.

CHAPTER III.

BUILDINGS OF JAUNPÛR.

But before speaking in detail of these buildings, now the sole memorials of the wealth of the powerful princes of Jaunpûr as also the evidence of their taste and culture, let us notice briefly those less important buildings which bear less conspicuously the marks of the dominant style. We are not indeed prepared to catalogue the many tombs of more or less pretension which from the time of Fîrûz to the present day have been built over former dwellers of Jaunpûr, nor to trace the fort Ibrâhîm built at Râî Barelî, or give a plan of the *kankar*-built palace erected by Vijayachandra II., and appropriated by the new dynasty, the remains of whose courts and halls occupy the centre of a lovely wood-clad knoll overhanging the Gûmtî some two miles west of the bridge. But not even the attractions of the later masjids will permit us to leave without notice the fort of Fîrûz or the masjid and halls with which it was decorated by Ibrâhîm Nâib Bârbak, Fîrûz's brother.

The fort is an irregular quadrangle on the north bank of the Gûmtî, formed by a stone wall built round an artificial earthen mound. Externally the walls are of considerable height, but as the mound occupies only the eastern half, their height from the level of the fort within is not uniform. Without, too, the higher ground on the side next the town made the northern wall always the most favourable to an escalading party. Besides a sally-port on the south-east face,—approached from within only by a steep passage, barely wide enough for an elephant, and cut through the artificial mound which might have been easily closed by a few cart-loads of earth,—the only entrance was by a gateway on the east, represented on Plate II,—unprotected by any outwork unless the walls of the city be regarded in that light—which doubtless existed, though there is no trace left of them. This building is 46′ 4″ high, 43′ 8″ wide at the base, and 40′ 3″ along the top, giving a slope to the walls of 1′ 8½″ each. On both sides of the entrance are large projecting piers connected by a lofty stone archway, and divided into four storeys by ornamented string mouldings. In the face of each storey is an arched recess containing an inner panel having a cusped head ornamented with *patera* and bell. Over the recess is a flat stone lintel incised with ornament. The gable wall under the main arch is pierced by a small arched opening, below which is a small bracketed cornice. Below this is another archway springing from moulded capitals crowning the jambs at the angles of the entrance. The lower part of the gateway is strengthened by a heavy plinth of similar design to that round the east entrance to the Atala masjid. The top is embattled and loopholed. In depth the gateway is about 16′ 1″, and on each side of the entrance leading to the fort is a small low chamber, 3′ 8″ by 4′ 7″ and 7′ 10″ high.

On the north and south side the gate is guarded by round loopholed bastions much wider at the base than above, and on the east face they have bartisans resting on moulded corbels.

The fort had more than once been carried by bold assailants burning the gate, before Munim Khân, Khân Khânân, built an outer court of brick with a fine gateway of stone adorned with *Káshâní* work,[1] whose chambers were never finished.

The main block of this gateway measures 37′ 6″ by 28′ 6″, but on the south side a wing has been added 27′ 0″ by 8′ 0″, which contains a staircase leading to an upper chamber over the entrance and which measures 34′ 1″ by 14 1½″. The walls are massive and thicker on the front than in the rear. On each side of the entrance is a deep recess 7′ 11″ by 12′ 7″, half-domed, with a vestibule between them measuring 14′ 9″ by 14′ 10½″ and crowned by a flat stone cupola. From outside the gateway resembles one of the great propylons in front of the masjids, the walls batter upwards, and the general design is the same. It is 36′ 8″ high.

The central portion stands back somewhat from the main face, and in it a large arch has been introduced, the spandrils over which are enriched by encaustic tile-work. Below this arch is a smaller one, 9′ 7″ to the springing and 7′ 10″ to the crown by 11 feet wide, through which access is gained to the courtyard. The space between the two arches is filled in with masonry, and the centre is pierced by an arched opening below which runs a small string moulding breaking up what otherwise would be plain field of ashlaring. The top of the gateway is crowned by a slight cornice, the frieze of which is composed of a flat glazed band of floral ornamentation in blue and yellow.

The space on each side of the main arch is divided into five storeys, and in each is inserted a deep arched niche or recess, 3′ 6″ in width and 5′ 2″ in height, all of which are highly ornamented. They are enclosed in architraves, the faces of which are enriched with carving: that of the second storey being carved with a Saracenic pattern, and that of the third storey is ornamented with a cheveron device in colour, while the others are embellished with a hexagonal and diamond pattern filled in with blue and yellow colours. The spandrils are similarly treated. The backs have cusped arches relieved by the bell ornament so frequently met with throughout the Jaunpûr buildings. Of the room over the entrance little remains save the jambs of the window and door openings and a few feet of the walls.

On the whole, the structure is in a fair state of preservation and with a small outlay might be repaired. The police now occupy it and the adjoining quarters, and let us therefore hope that some little care and attention will be bestowed on this old example of what military architecture used to be in India.

Fîrûz used the ruined temples of an earlier creed as quarries—and therein he was largely imitated by later princes—in obtaining materials for his new works. To what an extent Fîrûz drew on the ruins would hardly be believed by one who saw only the smooth walls standing, but when the towers were blown up in 1859, the inner face of nearly every stone bore carvings which had apparently made parts of Brâhmanical temples; in the walls remaining such carved blocks are not rare, the carvings being generally revealed by accident, yet sometimes it has been worked in as an ornament, as in the gateway the niches—which relieve the eastern face—are ornamented with bands, in one of which, not 12 feet long, may be counted seven distinct patterns.

Within the walls all is now desolation, and despite the lovely view, rich in the

[1] The practice of covering brick-work with raised ornamentation in green glazed tiles was introduced into India from Kâshân, a town in *Írân*; hence the word *kâshâní* or *káshí* means also green colour.

PLATE II

JAUNPUR EAST GATE OF FORT

charms of wood and water, unrivalled in the plains of India, a visit to it affords little pleasure. The destruction of the towers on the southern face and of that pretty building on the south-west— the Chahal Sitûn, the last habitable of Ibrâhîm's works—is to be lamented chiefly indeed as ruining the external beauty; but within no traces are left of the garden, and the rank jangal grass and that shrub whose lustrous copper-coloured leaves seem always evidence of long and utter neglect, suggest a strong desire that, if the rich local funds of the city can do nothing for the fort to which it and they owed their greatness, the despairing proposal of Khair-ad-dîn might be approved, and the area be made over to market-gardeners whose cultivation would at all events keep it clean. Not less conspicuous for the surrounding desolation are Ibrâhîm's spacious baths, still apparently capable of easy repair, and the masjid which served as a cathedral till the completion of the noble Atala.

The masjid of Ibrâhîm Nâib Bârbak measures externally 130 feet by 22, and is divided into three chambers by two lateral walls. The central one measures 37′ 5″ by 14′ 10″, and is roofed by three low-plastered domes of the Bengali type. The room on each side is 40′ 1″ by 18′ 10″, and is 8′ 2″ in height, and each is divided into five bays in depth and two in breadth. The outer row of pillars is double, of various designs, and no two columns measure exactly the same. From the back and two side enclosing walls pilasters project, ranging with the columns, but none are attached to the north and south sides of the lateral walls forming the central chamber as indicated on General Cunningham's plan.[1] The west wall is recessed between the bays, and the recess or *mihrâb* in the fourth bay in the southern arcade is emphasized by angle colonnettes, as is also the middle one in the central apartment.

The columns of which the arcades are composed are without bases and vary in design, and it is evident they have been wrought into a façade for which they were never intended. They have been set up at random; capitals inserted upside down, and bases used as caps. Some are octagonal, some square, others octagonal below, sixteen-sided in the middle and round above. One shaft on the north enclosing-wall is somewhat peculiar, being hexagonal in form and wrought on each face through its length, with a cheveron design. Most of the shafts are divided into two parts by broad bands, some octagonal, some square, and others circular and moulded. The capitals also vary in design and are double, the upper consisting of a bracket sur-capital which supports the architraves upon which the flat slabs of stone forming the ceiling rest. There is nothing interesting in the external façade, which is of cement.

The central apartment is elevated somewhat and measures 24′ 0″ in height, and stands 2′ 6″ above the arched entrances on each side leading to the central and domed area which rises some 7′ 6″ over the low arcades on each side. On each side of the central arch has been introduced a tapered octagonal stone of which the shaft is 36 feet high and moulded at the top.

The spandrils over the arch are plain with the exception of a small *patera* in the centre of each. The frieze is divided into three flat panels and is surmounted by a plain projecting cornice and embattled parapet. The plastered vaults and shallow ornamentation of the middle chamber raise a suspicion that it is not as its founder left it. The western range of pillars is closed by a plastered brick wall with niches. The pillars

[1] Cunningham's *Archæological Reports*, Vol. XI, Plate XXXI.

have certainly, the flat roofs probably, been taken from some Buddhist or Hindû temple, possibly from some of those at Zafarâbâd, which supplied most of the materials of the fort.

The following Arabic inscription, No. VII, is over the *mihrâb* of the central hall. The characters are plain Arabic ones and well preserved.

خالدين فيها و يكفر عنهم سيئاتهم و كان ذلك عند الله فوزا عظيما و يعذب المنافقين و المنافقات

و المشركين و المشركات الظانين بالله ظن

"(*The righteous*) ever live in Paradise; their evil doings are obliterated, and they are endowed with the best gift of God; and the wavering-minded individuals and polytheists who doubt the existence of God, are subjected to torments and punishment." [*Qurân*, Sûrah Fatḥ.]

About 27 feet in front of the middle of the southern wing stands the Lâṭ, or *minâr*, apparently wholly unaltered from the date of its erection, the Arabic inscription on which assigns the building of the masjid to **Ibrâhîm Nâib Bârbak**. Its octagonal base rises in five steps to the height of some 4 feet 6 inches; the upper face of this base gives little room for anything but the pillar, which is first square, then octagonal, then round, rising with its upper capital some 40 feet from the terrace of the masjid on which it stands.

The inscription No. VIII[1] runs in six lines round the upper half of the octagonal section; lines 2, 3, and 5 are partly defaced. The inscription is written in Arabic and in very fine Tughrâ characters. The *lacunæ* are filled up in brackets with the readings given by Khair-ad-dîn in his *Jaunpûrnâmah*.

بسم الله الرحمن الرحيم انما يعمر مساجد الله من آمن بالله و اليوم الآخر و قال رسول الله

صلى الله عليه و سلم من بنى مسجد الله تعالى اعطاه الله تعالى بكل شبر × ×

× × × × × ملائكته و محمد رسول الله تعالى م × × × × × × نجات ابدا

× × × × × × × × × سلطان سلاطين عالم عادل با ذل شهريار اعظم مالك

رقاب الامم مولى ملوك العرب و العجم مظهر كلمة الله العليا المتمسك بالعروة الوثقى الناظر لدين الله

الحافظ لبلاد الله ذو الامن و الامان لاهل ايمان وارث ملك سليمان × عالم × ابو المظفر فيروز شاه

السلطان خلد الله ملكه و سلطنته و بزمان ملك ملوك الشرق و الصين سلطان السلاطين ناصر الغزاة

الموحدين عمدة الامام عدة الايام سپهكش زمان الغ اعظم نايب سلطان يديم الله معاليه بشرف كار

فرماي اين عاليمقام مشرف گشت اين ملك نيكو سيرت صافي اعتقاد باتمام بناء خير جهد تمام فرمود

بماه ذو القعده معظم و بسال هجري نبوي ثمانه و سبعين و سبعمايته

[1] This inscription was first published by the late Dr. Blochmann in the *Proceedings of the Asiatic Society of Bengal* for January 1875. Some portions of the second line have been omitted by him, as probably the rubbings sent to him by General Cunningham were defective.

"In the name of God, the merciful, the clement. 'Surely, he will build the masjids of God, who believes in God and the last day.' [*Qurán.*] And the Prophet—blessings upon him!—says: 'He who builds a masjid for God, will receive from God (*a house in Paradise in lieu of every stone and beam used in the masjid.' So, according to the holy writ and the word of the Prophet, peace upon him, which refers to the erection of masjids, in hope of going to Paradise and gaining salvation, the erection of this masjid in the fort was ordered by*) the mighty, the high, the king of the kings of the world, the just, the generous, and great ruler, the lord of the necks of nations, the master of the kings of Arabia and Persia, who professes the exalted creed and seizes the firm handle (*of the sword*), who watches over God's faith, protects God's lands and defends God's servants, who gives the faithful peace and security, the heir of the kingdom of Solomon (*strengthened by the grace of God*), **Abûl Muzaffar Fîrûz Shâh**, the king,—may God perpetuate his kingdom and his rule!—and in the time of the Malik of the Maliks of the East and of China, the king of the kings, the helper of the warring monotheists, the excellent Imâm, the hope of the age, the general of the present time (*the best noble*), the great **Ulugh Ibrâhîm Nâib Bârbak**, the king,—may God continue to him his high position!—(*this building*) received the distinction of being erected, and this prince, whose walk of life is good, and whose faith is pure, exerted himself to the utmost to finish this religious edifice in the exalted month Zil Qa'dâh and in the year 778 of the flight of the Prophet, upon whom rest God's blessings." [*April 1376.*]

Khair-ad-dîn has given the date A.H. 798, reading *tisâin* (90) instead of *sabâin* (70). The month Zil Qa'dâh seems to have been a favourite with the Jaunpûr rulers, as it is recorded with care that the dedication of the Atala masjid took place in the same month. **Ibrâhîm Nâib Bârbak** is stated by Zîa-ad-dîn Barnî to have been **Fîrûz Shâh's** brother,—see *Shams-i-Sirâj Afîf.*

Outside the fine gateway, built by Khân Khânân Munim Khân, stands a monolith opposite the kotwâl's house, on which the following Persian inscription (No. IX) is recorded. The Lâṭ is 6′ high and rests on a round base 2′ 5″ high; the inscribed space measures 2′ 8″ by 4″; the inscription consists of seventeen lines of Persian prose :—

بسم الله الرّحمن الرّحيم

رجه يوميه سادات بينوا و غيره غربا

انچه بر آمدني ساير جونپور مقرر است

هميشه ميماند هرکس که حاکم و کوتوال و قبضه‌دار

جاري از حضور شده باشد

رجه يوميه آنرا موافق مجراى حضورش

ميداده باشد تاکم يا زياده نشود و طمعي چيزي

در مذکور بردیا در اقربا و وارث و خويشان

نيز دهد آنرا قسم خدا و رسول صلی الله عليه و

پنجتن پاک و دوازده امام و دوازده معصوم است

و اگر سنّي باشد اورا قسم زيارات است

و هندو را قسم رام و گنگاجي است
و اگر باین طلاق باز گردد به لعنت خدا و رسول ص
گرفتار گردد پیش الله تعالی بروز قیامت
رو سیاه شده سر گروه دوزخیان باشد
مرقوم هشتم ربیع اول سنه ۱۱۸۰ هجري
باني این کار خیر سید علي منیر خان بهادر

1. In the name of God, the merciful, the clement.
2. The daily stipend to helpless Sa'ids and other poor persons,
3. Which is fixed upon the revenue of Jaunpûr, may continue.
4. Every governor, kotwâl, district officer and commander of forces,
5. Appointed by His Majesty [*Asaf-ad-daula, of Oudh*],
6. May pay their daily stipend according to the rate prescribed by His Majesty,
7. So that it should be not more or less. Should any covet a part
8. Of the said stipend or hand over to his relatives, heirs, or inmates,
9. He is prohibited by God, Prophet, may the blessings of God be upon him!
10. By the five pious beings, twelve imâms, and twelve innocents;
11. And if he be a Sunnî, he is prohibited by the eminent saints,
12. And a Hindû, upon Râma and Gaṅgâ.
13. If any disregard this oath, may he suffer the imprecation of God and Prophet, may the blessings of God be upon him!
14. And in the presence of God at the resurrection,
15. Forego the hellish individuals in disgrace.
16. Written on the 8th Rabi-al-awwal 1180 Hijra. [A.D. 1766.]
17. Sa'îd 'Alî Munîr Khân Bahâdur is the beginner of this good deed.

CHAPTER IV.

THE ATALA MASJID.

But the Fort Masjid of Ibrâhîm Nâib Bârbak, the earliest building, is not to be reckoned among the chief attractions of Jaunpûr, those noble masjids, unique in style and unrivalled in grandeur by such as depend, for their beauty, only on elegance of design and elaboration of material and not on the facile glory of rare marbles and bright enamels.

An extract from Mr. Fergusson's description of the Atala masjid[1] will give an idea of the general features of the Jaunpûr style. "It consists," he says, "of a courtyard, on the western side of which is situated a range of buildings, the central one covered by a dome, in front of which stands a gate-pyramid or propylon of almost Egyptian manner and outline. This gate-pyramid by its elevation supplied the place of a minaret which none of these masjids possess. The three sides of the courtyard were surrounded by colonnades, on each face was a handsome gateway. These Jaunpûr examples are well worthy of illustration and in themselves possess a simplicity and grandeur not often met with in this style. An appearance of strength, moreover, is imparted to them by their sloping walls."

This extract will show that the special characteristics of the Jaunpûr style is the lofty propylon with sloping walls hiding a single dome (see Plate III); and it would be well to have some idea of the causes which led at this place to the adoption of this plan, so original, so quickly perfected and hardly imitated elsewhere. Did we know, as we can never hope to know, which was called forth first, the dome or propylon, we should be able to guess the object each was to answer. For, while the dome is undoubtedly the most imposing covering for a single chamber, it seems, at least when seen from without, to overpower a room whose walls are not proportionally lofty; and it is hard to fancy how the effect of any building could be pleasing where a dome covered the centre of a simple oblong. If, then, for the sake of an imposing internal roof to a central chamber, the founder wished to build a dome, and if with his desire to utilise material existing in abundance at hand, he was somewhat cramped in his choice of the height of his building, no great ingenuity would be wanted to make him think of proportionally elevating the central portion of his façade, turning his minarets, if he had planned any, into abutments, and filling the intervening arch with a rich screen which should hide the dome. This seems the true theory. For the idea of the dome must surely have come first. The bold façade standing alone can have been satisfactory only when viewed from directly in front; from every other point it would have seemed purposeless, from behind worse than purposeless. Yet, though it had been possible to view it only in the most advantageous way, from the direct front, few would dream of building a façade 75 feet high and 55 feet wide at the base. And so we would claim for the

[1] *History of Indian and Eastern Architecture*, pp. 522-524.

Pathân architects of Jaunpûr the honour of being the first in India to make domes and their adjuncts an imposing part of a range of buildings.

The plan of the Atala masjid confirms this theory. Here the architect has thought the western wings wanted emphasizing, and has done this by constructing small domes half-way between the centre dome and the cloisters of the north and south sides of the court; but though these domes are certainly not so large as to seem to crush the substructure, he has hidden each behind a proportionate propylon. But the Zafarâbâd masjid seems at first sight to make against the theory; for while it certainly never had a dome, it has had a large arch between two piers giving a façade as lofty as that of the Atala. But the cases are not at all similar: first, in the arch at Zafarâbâd the substructure is stone to above the level of the roof, and the arch has been of stone, but the upper half of the piers is of brick. Again, the façade of the Jaunpûr style has the arch closed with a pierced screen; the little remains of the spring of the Zafarâbâd arch do not seem to have any traces of the inner or recessed arch which framed the screen; and if it ever had this inner arch and screen, it alone of all has lost it.

These masjids are constructed entirely of stone, mortar, and concrete. The walls are of ashlar masonry, set with fine and well wrought joints. Internally throughout, the columns, roofs and domes are of stone, whilst the exterior of the domes and roofs, parapets and floors is floated with cement. The roof over the cloisters and the chambers on either side of the great dome and principal propylon are formed of flat slabs of stone running at right angles to horizontal architraves, themselves supported by bracket corbels springing from the capitals of square pillars.

The plates, XL and XLI, giving different masons' marks,[1] found on the columns and stone ashlaring of the buildings, sufficiently show that the materials were brought from Hindû and Buddhist temples in the neighbourhood and that Hindûs were the workmen.

First in order comes the Atala masjid, one of the earliest specimens of the Jaunpûr style. In point of size, it stands about midway between the Jâmi and Lâl Darwâza masjids. In the beginning of 1860, the fall of the outer arch had reduced the square and noble façade to a rich screen flanked by two ruinous pinnacles; but it has now been completely 'restored' at the cost of Munshi Hâidar Husain of Jaunpûr. It was built on the site of an ancient temple of Ataladevî said by Khair-ad-dîn to have been erected, but more probably only further appropriated, in Saṁvat 1416 (A.D. 1358), by Râjâ Jayachandra II. of Zafarâbâd for the reception of his favourite image, and how largely it is indebted to its predecessor may be judged from the extract from Mr. Fergusson given below. This temple caught Fîrûz's eye when he was building his Fort, but his attempt to destroy it was so violently opposed by the Hindûs of the neighbourhood, that after much bloodshed, he was compelled to enter into a written compact which bound him and his successors to leave other temples untouched and not further to injure this, though closing it to Hindû rites. To this compact produced before him, Ibrâhîm paid small attention, filling with consternation those who had trusted to it, by a very plain statement that the propriety of making agreements and the propriety of keeping them when made, varied with the power of the parties. Yet he is said to have spared the gate of Ataladevî, only hewing away the Hindû carvings: there is now no trace of such a building.

[1] See *Indian Antiquary*, vol. IV, pp. 302-305, vol. VII, pp. 295-298; *The Builder* of the 26th June 1869, Plate I, Nos. 1-6.

Photo-etching
Survey of India Offices, Calcutta, December

Brief as Mr. Fergusson's description is, we shall do well to quote it: "Of the three masjids remaining at Jaunpûr," he says, "the Atala masjid is the most ornate and most beautiful. The colonnades surrounding its court are four aisles in depth, the outer columns of which are double square pillars, as are also those adjoining the interior of the court. The three intermediate rows are single square columns. This is altogether so like an Indian arrangement that I at one time was half inclined to agree with Baron Hügel and fancy that this was really an old Buddhist monastery. Its gateways, however, which are purely Saracenic, are the principal ornaments of the outer court, and the western face is adorned by three propylons similar to that of the Lâl Darwâza, but richer and more beautiful, while its interior domes and roofs are superior to any other specimen of Muhammadan art I am acquainted with of so early an age."

The number of the colonnade aisles, however, is five instead of four; but in this passage we find raised the most interesting of the questions concerning the antiquities of Jaunpûr, *viz.*, how much of this building is really Ibrâhîm's work. On the strength of the Saracenic gates and the true masjid, Mr. Fergusson assigns all to that prince, while he understands Baron Hügel, on the strength of the plan of the colonnades, to assign all to the older rulers of the subject country. But we have historical evidence that a demolition and desecration begun by Fîrûz Shâh was carried much further by Ibrâhîm, and therefore the whole of the existing building is certainly not Bauddha work. Indeed, there is little evidence that they ever built domes anywhere, and the abundant use of what is popularly called Buddhist ornament may be accounted for by the fact that the materials of older buildings were largely used, that the workmen employed were doubtless natives of the country,[1] and that the new comers, possessing no national style of ornament, naturally have accepted and followed the rich ornament they found. But, on the other hand, there was no reason why Ibrâhîm should throw down more than either he considered as defiled by the rites he was supplanting or which stood in the way of any new arrangement. And Bauddha and early Hindû architecture lends itself freely to partial demolitions and reconstructions. Made up of isolated portions, using no arches, which if beautiful are also the most destructive of all structural expedients, it allows of the fall, without risk to other portions, of any piece of roofing or even of single pillars. Ibrâhîm might therefore have demolished any side or part of a side of the court and joined his new work on to the old without fear of any destructive "set." Notwithstanding this, however, it must be granted from an examination of the structure as it now stands that Mr. Fergusson, rather than Baron Hügel, is correct, and that no part of the Buddhist cloisters were left untouched by Ibrâhîm, when he replaced the *cella* by his splendid masjid, built the gateways that now so much ornament the otherwise bare enclosure, which he at least reconstructed.

The archways over the transoms of the small doorways leading from the lower to the upper cloisters are mostly filled in with stone trellis-work, and there remains evidence that at one time the ends of the upper cloisters were also closed by stone lattice screens.

Black marble has been largely used in the decoration of the interior of the grand dome, principally of the arches, mihrâbs, architraves, &c., &c.

Formerly the pointed window openings in the screen gable wall of the great arch

[1] See inscriptions Nos. XIII and XV.

of the propylon were filled in with trellis-work which, much to its detriment, has been omitted in the recent restoration.

The Plates.

The drawing (Plate IV)[1] shows that the ground plan of the building consists of a quadrangle surrounded on the north, south, and east sides by cloisters two storeys high, with the masjid itself on the west.

The masjid with its principal propylon, which is highly decorated (Plates III and VII) and supported on either side by a similar but smaller one, forms the most prominent feature of the building. It is divided into five compartments: a central room at the back of the principal propylon, an oblong room of one storey 62′ 0″ by 28′ 8″ on either side, and two low rooms in two storeys in each corner. Originally these were separated from the rest of the building by stone screen-work of which portions still exist.[2] Access to these chambers is gained by private doors in the external walls. They were used as *zanâna* chapels. The ceilings over the upper floor are divided into panels which are richly carved, formed by stone beams crossing at right angles from column to column. The external walls on the south and north sides respectively are pierced with window openings filled in with stone trellis-work. The west walls are divided into bays by projecting square pilasters in the centre of which recesses or niches are inserted.

The planning of the central room is somewhat peculiar, and although oblong in form it is roofed by a hemispherical dome. It measures 29′ 6″ in width by 35′ 0″ in length. On studying the construction of the dome it is found that the difference in the dimensions is rectified by large projecting corbels from the four piers in the side walls, and from the corners, so as to make the portion to be roofed by the dome a square (Plates IV and IX). The angles of the square are cut off in the usual way and an octagon formed, which in its turn is developed into a sixteen-sided figure, and upon this the cupola of the dome is carried. The interior of the dome is constructed of stone, whilst the outside is of cement only.

In the room behind each smaller propylon, there is a hexagonal opening covered by a dome.

The courtyard is gained by massive entrance gateways of stone (Plates IV, VI, XIV, and XV) in the centre of the north, south, and east façades. On either side of each of these entrances is a stone staircase leading to the upper cloisters. In front of the north and south entrances on the courtyard side there is an octagonal room in the cloisters one storey high and roofed by a dome. The pillars are formed by placing two Hindû shafts one above the other to gain the requisite height (Plate XIX, fig. 1). The domes are panelled on the inside and enriched both externally and internally by decorated cornices.

The cloisters on the ground-floor are three aisles in depth. Around the outside of cloisters is a row of rooms and beyond them a veranda carried on coupled square columns. The portion of the courtyard in front of the masjid is paved with stone and forms the praying-ground.

[1] The following paragraphs to the end of this chapter are chiefly written by Mr. E. W. Smith.—J. B.

[2] Section through small propylon and Plate IV, fig. 1.

The upper plan (Plate V) differs somewhat from the lower. The space occupied by the rooms in front of the cloisters and the veranda beyond is roofed over and the whole breadth divided into five open aisles by columns of which the two outer lines are square and coupled, whilst the four inner rows are in some cases octagonal and in others round. The columns on the lower floor are all square and those on the outer rows are coupled. The roof over the masjid is shown on this plan. This has been done to mark the distinction between it and the *zanána* courts, which are two storeys in height. The plan of the domes at the back of the smaller propylons is also indicated. Corridors surround the grand dome on the east, north and south sides, and staircases lead to the top of the propylon in front. The corridors are divided into bays, four of which, two on the south and two on the north side, are domed, whilst the remaining have flat decorated roofs. From the *zanána* court on the south-west angle of the building a staircase leads to the roof, where the top of it is surmounted by a small dome.

The drawing (Plate VI, figure 1) shows the difference between the entrances on the north and south sides and that on the east. To the rear of those entrances is a dome, but not so at the rear of this. The manner in which the domes are supported is shown and the steps leading to the top of the gateway. On each side of the south entrance is a staircase leading to the upper cloister. The screen-work enclosing the *zanána* court is shown in the distance at the end of the chamber behind the dome. This and the other gateways closely resemble in outline the propylon of the masjid, but they are of no great elevation,—see for instance Plates VI and XV. Khair-ad-dîn having forcibly lamented the violence of Sikandar Lodî, and especially his destruction of the eastern gate of *every* masjid, one feels some surprise at seeing it here only slightly injured by time (see Plate XV). Over every gate is a large slab which has borne a Persian inscription; on *this* gate the slab has been replaced by a new one: on the southern and northern gates the bars around the different lines may be traced, but few characters of the inscription are legible; one preserved, however, in the *Ahwálát Jaunpúr wáh Sulṭán Hindústán* and thence extracted in Khair-ad-dîn's *Jaunpúrnámah*, gives the date of the completion of the masjid—Zil Qa'dâh A.H. 821=A.D. 1418,—but mentions among Ibrâhîm's titles his youthful office of Nâib 'Atabûk 'Azîm.[1] As will be stated hereafter, Fîrûz Shâh appropriated the temple of Ataladevî in A.D. 1376, and Ibrâhîm finished the masjid in A.D. 1408. See inscriptions X, XIII–XVIII.

Plate VI, Fig. 2, illustrates the northern façade. In the centre is the gateway or entrance to the courtyard or piazza (for detail see Plate XIV). The cloisters, both upper and lower, with the veranda in front of the lower rooms (originally used as shops), are ranged on either hand. A side view of the eastern entrance, also of the principal propylon, is shown with the grand dome behind. The *zanána* court appears on the left-hand side. The private entrance referred to above, in connection with Plate IV and the trellis-work in the window openings on each side of it, are indicated. The upper portion has been lately "restored" in cement, but unfortunately without regard to the architecture of the other portion of the fabric. The opposite court on the south-west angle remains as originally designed, and if it had only been intelligently studied by the *conservators*, the result might easily have been made far more pleasing than it now is.

[1] I am unable to give the text of this inscription according to the '*Ahwálát Jaunpúr*, as it was impossible for me to obtain a loan of the only existing manuscript from Qâzî Khalîl, Honorary Magistrate of Jaunpûr.

The height of the propylon shown on Plates VI, VII, VIII, is 75′ 0″, the width across the base is 54′ 7″, whilst that across the top is only 47′ 0″, showing a batter in the walls of 3′ 9″ on either side. Fergusson notes this peculiarity, though on a cursory glance and to the uneducated eye it may not at first sight be observed.

The exterior of the staircase is divided longitudinally by decorated string-courses or label mouldings into six storeys, the second, third, fourth, and fifth of which are embellished with recessed arches or niches enclosed in ornamented architraves. The whole of the centre portion is arched and the upper part of the screen gable wall pierced by openings, originally filled in with screen-work, which in the restoration was unfortunately omitted. In the lower portion are openings leading to the central area of the masjid.

The half section on Plate VII shows the peculiar arrangement of the dome above referred to. The area, it will be observed from the ground plan, is oblong on the floor, and this has to be reduced first to a square by corbelling, and then to an octagon. The octagonal sides of the drum are elaborately treated, and over this is a sixteen-sided section from which springs the cupola divided into enriched panels by projecting ribs of dark or black coloured marble. The interior height of this dome from the floor is 56 feet 2 inches.

As is universally the case, the *mimbár*, or pulpit, stands to the right or north side of the principal *mihráb*.

The section passes through the central arch leading into the north wing; and above it cuts through the arcade surrounding the base of the dome on the north, east, and south sides. The architraves over the openings and recesses, as well as the bands around the arches, and the *mihrábs*, are executed in black slate or coarse marble.

The massive pieces of masonry guarding the entrance to the dome and containing the staircases are 30′ 0″ apart, the inner walls of course vertical: the batter on the outer and side walls is plainly visible, commencing above the foundation course which rises square some 19″ over the level of the praying-ground. The façade stands back 9′ 6″ from the base of the piers. In 1860 the main arch of the propylon had fallen, and the remaining façade consisted of the doorways with a rich screen above, but it has now been restored to somewhat of its former character. The line which divides this façade on a level with the roof of the cloisters Fergusson calls, after the fashion of Gaur, the *Bádsháh-ká-Takht*, or the king's throne,—a term which does not seem to be used here.

The central portion of Plate VIII shows the back of the principal propylon and the exterior of the grand dome. On either side stand the small propylons with the domes over the masjid in rear, and on the right and left of these appear the domes over the north and south entrances.

The section on Plate IX is drawn through the centre of the chamber under the grand dome and shows the groining and reveal of the window over the principal *mihráb*, the aperture of which is filled in with stone trellis-work; beyond is given the half elevation of the lower portion of the chamber. The lower openings lead to the oblong arcade on the north side of the masjid; those above open on to the corridor (Plate V) surrounding the dome on three of its sides. At one time they were filled in with stone screens. The system of corbelling devised to reduce the space to be domed over to a square is shown here. The arches are four-centered, slightly stilted and ornamented with cusping on their soffits;

they are supported on angle shafts composed of two turned balusters—top and bottom—and a small panelled octagonal pillar separated by carved dies. The outer face of the arches and architraves is of black marble richly carved. The spandrils are ornamented with lotus rosettes, and those in the upper arches are panelled in addition. The entire chamber forms a most artistic, elaborate, and effective piece of work, the full beauty of which is now unfortunately marred and hidden by the numerous coats of whitewash which have been administered from time to time by ignorant and misguided conservators.

On account of the beauty of the side elevation of the central entrance, a detail of it has been given in Plate X. The lower portion has been executed in stone, whilst nearly the whole of the upper part is of black marble. Highly ornamented stone corbels project to carry the stone lintels bridging the openings. The soffit is of one slab of stone and forms an elaborate piece of carved ceiling-work (see Plate XI). The small columns or balusters to the arched recesses in the side of the entrance are of black marble; a detail of them as well as the bands at A and B is given in figures 2, 3. Portions of this elaborate piece of work are decayed, particularly the backgrounds of the recesses, which were originally carved and of which small fragments are still extant.

The ceiling to the entrance of the masjid under the great dome (Plate XI) has just been referred to. The panels are eight-cornered with intervening crosses and are filled in with small *pateræ*. In the centre is a large *patera* in bold relief. The whole is of one piece of stone.

On reference to the ground plan (Plate IV) the position of the principal *mihrâb* (Plate XII) under the great dome will be seen to be exactly in the centre of the main west wall of the masjid, from the face of which it is recessed 4′ 4″. It is square in plan; the upper portion is domical (Fig. 2) and ribbed. The architrave encasing it and the band around the arch is of black marble and beautifully carved. To the north of the *mihrâb* stands the *mimbâr* or pulpit. The whole forms one of the most charming pieces of work to be seen in the building.

In the centre of the tympanum in the arched recess on either side of the principal *mihrâb* under the grand dome is carved a large *patera* (Plate XIII) in three tiers in high relief, and the field around it is embellished by raised carving of a radiating, repeating, arabesque design made up principally of moulded trefoiled zigzags filled in with rosettes and standing on an elaborate and intricate background of tracery studded with stars.

The height of the north gateway given in half elevation in Plate XIV is 34 feet 6 inches from the ground-level, with a base of 41′ 7″, and a breadth at the top of 38′ 0″, showing a batter of 1′ 10″ on each side. It projects 7′ 1″ in front of the veranda. The same treatment is applied to the entrances on the east and south façades, which resemble more or less the large propylon in front of the masjid proper. The screen wall over the inner arch is panelled, and on the centre the remains of a Persian inscription are to be seen. The southern gateway is similar to this in design, but that on the east side is more ornate.

The front elevation of the north gateway given on Plate VI, Fig. 2, is shown in detail on Plate XIV. The section (Plate XIX, Fig. 1) is through the vestibule leading to the octagonal chamber on the courtyard side which is roofed by a dome. Above the cornice the octagonal form is superseded by one of sixteen sides upon which springs the cupola of the dome. The whole is supported by square pillars one storey in height formed by placing two Hindû shafts one upon another, the capping of which carries the corbelling on which the dome rests.

Of the three entrances to the masjid the eastern one is the largest and most beautiful, and in general design somewhat resembles the propylon in front of the grand dome (see Plates XV and VII). The central portion is considerably recessed and spanned by a four-centred arch of ogee form, and the spandrils over which are panelled and ornamented by *pateræ*. The upper part of the tympanum or gable is pierced by an opening, whilst the lower is divided into panels by bands of exquisitely-carved fretwork. The whole is supported on a massive lintel, chamfered on the top and bottom, which rests on the jambs of the arched entrance to the vestibule leading to the cloister. The heavy masonry on either side of the main archway is broken up by richly-ornamented horizontal string-courses or table-mouldings, and in the storeys thus formed are introduced arched niches or recesses, the backgrounds of which were at one time beautifully carved. The arches of these niches are cusped and supported on angle shafts composed of two small balusters separated by a carved die, and the whole is enclosed by an enriched architrave slightly projecting from the face of the masonry. The top of the gateway is crowned by an elaborate and bold cornice of which a torus moulding is the most prominent member. The entire structure stands on a massive podium or base, laden with mouldings—bold but effective, owing to the play of light and shade caused by the deep undercutting of the members.

Plate XVI illustrates the propylon standing on the south side of the grand dome, that on the north being the counterpart to it. The central portion ranges in a line with the outer row of columns of the masjid proper, and is supported on each side by tower-like structures which are connected by a stilted arch carried on corbels. The screen wall beneath is supported on lintels upheld by heavy corbels; the centre of the upper portion is recessed and pierced by an opening over which is turned a cusped arch supported on small double-baluster shafts. The towers are pierced by openings which lead, like the central entrance, to the oblong chamber beyond. They are surmounted by stilted cusped arches, the inner springing from the top of pretty, slender, twisted and turned shafts. Three feet above the smaller entrances runs a profusely-decorated horizontal string-course dividing the tower into two storeys. The otherwise heavy appearance of the upper storey is overcome by introducing into the lower portion a large square panel, the field of which is carved with a raised geometrical device (Plate XVII), and into the upper an oblong recess filled in at the top with a cusped arch resting on angle shafts similar in design to those in the entrance below.

These panels—illustrated in Plate XVII—in the small propylons on each side of the great dome, stand just above the string-course over the small side entrances of the propylon. The centre portion is set back considerably from the outer face of the panel, and carved on it in relief is a peculiar geometrical device formed by inserting two squares in a circle, and joining the third points in succession of the eight thus formed on the circumference, this produces eight trapeziums which enclose a rosette, the whole being comprised within a square panel with a double ovolo moulding, which in its turn is surrounded by a broad sunk border enriched by a band of continuous floral carving.

The whole of the west interior wall of the masjid is divided by piers into bays, and in the centre of each a *mihrâb* is formed,—those under the domes, especially that under the grand dome, being larger and of a more elaborate design. Over each is a window extending the whole depth of the wall, and filled in with trellis-work. With the exception of the windows lighting the *zanána* courts, there are no others in the entire building.

The depth of the *mihráb* under the small dome on the south side of the principal propylon (Plate XVIII) is 4′ 0″ (see also Plate IV and section on Plate VI, Fig. 1). Like those on the north side of the masjid, the central room is domed over, but all the remainder are linteled by stone beams.

The screen illustrated in Plates XIX, figure 2, and XXII, figure 1, is of stone, and stands at the west end of the upper northern cloister. It faces into the passage separating the cloisters from the *zanána* courts, and is divided into three bays, each of a separate design. A detail of one portion only is shown.

Fig. 1, Plate XX, gives a section through the cloister on the north side of the east gate. The lower storey is divided into three parts,—aisles, rooms used as shops in former times, and a veranda beyond. The upper floor has five aisles in depth and extends over the rooms and veranda below (Plates IV and V). The four inner lines of columns are mostly octagonal, but the outer rows on either side are square and coupled. Those on the ground-floor are all square, and the columns in the outer lines are coupled.

Fig. 2, Plate XX, shows the elevation of the cloister facing the court (for section, see Fig. 1). The columns are all square, and the outer row coupled. The wall at the back of the cloister separating it from the room on the exterior is panelled between the pilasters. These panels or recesses are set back about six inches from the main face of the wall and are arched.

Fig. 3.—Elevation facing the road and showing the openings to the rooms or shops with the veranda in front.

Fig. 5, Plate XX.—Detail of the inner row of columns on the upper floor. The base of the column is square, and upon it stands a shaft, octagonal below, sixteen-sided in the middle, and circular above. The capital is round and supports corbels carrying lintels which pass from column to column and support the roof. Fig. 4 gives a detail of the capital on the single columns in the aisles.

Fig. 1, Plate XXI.—Detail of the capitals over the columns on the upper storey facing the courtyard. The bracket shown only exists in a few instances, but at one time was general.

Fig. 2, Plate XXI, gives a detail of the capitals of the outer line of columns on the upper floor.

Fig. 3 gives a side elevation of the capitals on the square coupled columns on the ground-floor, facing the court.

The only remaining examples of what may possibly have been Buddhist columns in the masjid are shown on Plates XXI. Fig. 4, and XXIII, Figs. 1, 2, 3, and less probably the capitals on Plate XXII, Figs. 2 and 3; and if they are such they tend to prove the theory that at one time a Buddhist temple stood on the spot now occupied by the masjid. Dut they may quite as well, from anything in their style, have belonged to a Bráhmanical or Jaina temple. In the construction of the cloisters they have been re-used by the Muhammadan architect.

Like the outer drum of the dome the external cornice round the spring of the great dome (Plate XXIV, Fig. 1) is executed in stone, whilst the material employed for the external coating of the dome itself is cement. It is of a bold and massive design, and although on close inspection the mouldings appear coarse, they are very effective as seen from below. The crowning band encircling the dome is ornamented with pointed arcading and projects 1′ ½″ from the face of the dome. In the centre of each arch is a rosette carved in relief and under it a triangular leaf ornament. The mouldings below this band project 6½″ from the face, and are perfectly plain, with the exception of the lowest member, which is relieved by some projecting floral carving.

Like the drums and cornices of the other domes, the mouldings round the bases of the smaller domes (Plate XXIV, Fig. 2) are of stone, divided into three portions; the upper consisting of plain projecting pointed arcading with carved central rosettes; the middle, of a recessed band broken up by square panels, the angles of which are stepped; and the lower, of a string course made up of an ovolo band and a cyma with fillets below, all of which are uncarved.

Plate XXIV, Fig. 3, is a detail of the band and string-course running round the upper portion of the western exterior of the central room behind the grand propylon (see Plate VI). The band continues around the whole of the western façade and answers the purpose of a cornice. It is of stone, and owing to the deep undercutting and boldness of its members looks remarkably well in execution.

Inscriptions.

The following nine inscriptions have been found in the Ataladevî masjid; they prove that Fîrûz Shâh commenced the appropriation of the masjid in A.D. 1376, that Ibrâhîm Shâh finished the building in A.D. 1408, and that the masons employed were Hindûs.

Inscription No. X is written in Persian poetry, the metre being *Ramal*, in six lines, on a loose slab, measuring 1′ 2″ by 8″, found lying on the maulavi's pulpit (*mimbâr*) in the Atala masjid. The stone was thickly covered with the dust of ages, and required a good deal of clearing before the inscription was readable.

شکر مر حق را که عهد مملکت فیروز شاه

خسروي کامل به رافت اهل ادیانرا مدار

در زمان شست و پنج و هفتصد لشکري

غره شوال یکشنبه بوقت ساز وار

صاحب خیرات خواجه کامل خان جهان

کرد این مسجد بنای رهنمای هر دیار

1. Praise be to God! In the reign of **Fîrûz Shâh**,
2. Who is benevolently the repository of religious men,
3. In the year seven hundred and sixty-five Lsahkarî,
4. At an auspicious time, on Sunday the first Shâwâl,
5. The generous **Khwâja Kamâl Khân Jahân**,
6. Founded this masjid for the guidance of every country.

By order of the second **Khalîfa**, **Mughîra** led arms against India and conquered her as far as **Sindh** in the 13th Hijra, which is regarded as the commencement of the

Lashkarî era; hence 765 + 13 = 778 Hijra = 1376 A.D. This date is supported by another inscription, No. XIII, giving Samvat 1433 = A.D. 1376.

Inscription No. XI is written in excellent Tughrâ characters on a white marble slab measuring 4′ 9″ by 1′ 2″ on the top of the principal *mihrâb* in the centre hall (see Plate XII).

بِسْمِ اللّٰهِ الرَّحْمٰنِ الرَّحِيْمِ قَالَ اللّٰهُ تَعَالٰى اِنَّمَا يَعْمُرُ مَسَاجِدَ اللّٰهِ مَنْ اٰمَنَ بِاللّٰهِ وَ الْيَوْمِ الْاٰخِرِ

وَ اَقَامَ الصَّلٰوةَ وَ اٰتَى الزَّكٰوةَ وَلَمْ يَخْشَ اِلَّا اللّٰهَ فَعَسٰى اُولٰٓئِكَ اِنْ يَكُوْنَ مِنَ الْمُهْتَدِيْنَ وَ قَالَ النَّبِيُّ صَلَّى

اللّٰهُ عَلَيْهِ وَ سَلَّمَ مَنْ بَنٰى لِلّٰهِ مَسْجِدًا وَلَوْ كَفَحصِ قَطَاةٍ بَنَى اللّٰهُ لَهٗ بَيْتًا فِى الْجَنَّةِ

"In the name of God, the merciful, the clement. The Lord God has said: 'Surely he will erect masjids in honour of God who believes in God and the day of resurrection, who performs prayers and bestows charity, and fears none but God. It is hoped that he will rank among the righteous' [*Qurân*, Sûrah IX], and the Prophet—God bless him!—has said that 'if anybody builds a masjid in honour of God, even like the nest of the *qatah* (*a bird*), God makes a house for him in Paradise.'"

Inscription No. XII is written in Arabic characters on the right and left side of the oblong parallelogram of the inner arch of the *mihrâb*,—see Plate XI.

بِسْمِ اللّٰهِ الرَّحْمٰنِ الرَّحِيْمِ وَ بِهٖ نَسْتَعِيْنُ

لَا اِلٰهَ اِلَّا اللّٰهُ مُحَمَّدٌ رَسُوْلُ اللّٰهِ وَ بِهٖ نَسْتَعِيْنُ

اللّٰهُ لَا اِلٰهَ اِلَّا هُوَ الْحَيُّ الْقَيُّوْمُ لَا تَاْخُذُهٗ سِنَةٌ وَ لَا نَوْمٌ لَهٗ مَا فِى السَّمٰوٰتِ وَمَا فِى الْاَرْضِ مَنْ

ذَا الَّذِيْ يَشْفَعُ عِنْدَهٗ اِلَّا بِاِذْنِهٖ يَعْلَمُ مَا بَيْنَ اَيْدِيْهِمْ وَمَا خَلْفَهُمْ وَلَا يُحِيْطُوْنَ بِشَيْءٍ مِنْ عِلْمِهٖ اِلَّا بِمَا شَآءَ وَسِعَ

كُرْسِيُّهُ السَّمٰوٰتِ وَالْاَرْضَ وَلَا يَؤُدُهٗ حِفْظُهُمَا وَهُوَ الْعَلِيُّ الْعَظِيْمُ

"In the name of God, the merciful, the clement. From Him I solicit protection.

"There is no God but God and Muhammad is His Prophet. From Him I solicit protection.

"God! there is no God but He who is living and self-subsisting. Sleep and slumber do not seize Him. Every earthly and heavenly thing belongs to Him. Who can intercede with Him save His own permission? He knows their present and past and His knowledge does not come within their compass, except what He himself pleases. His throne extends over heaven and earth, and their preservation is not onerous to Him. He is the high, the mighty." [*Qurân*, Sûrah II.]

Inscription No. XIII is found on a stone near the first niche on the south side of the east gate; the characters are very large and deeply cut.

पटुमाग्मूत्रधरो वीसे ह्नसुत: ॥ सम्वत् १४३३ ॥

"The mason Paṭumân, the son of Vîsaihva, Saṁvat 1433 = A.D. 1376."

Inscription No. XIV, सम्वत् १४३५ ॥ records the date Saṁvat 1435 — A.D. 1378 on the third pillar of the fifth aisle, lower storey, north-east side; the whole pillar is adorned with an exquisite band of flowers.

Inscription No. XV is engraved in three lines on the right jamb of the northern door outside.

[1] सम्वत् १४६४ समये

[2] सूत्रधार पदुमवि:

[3] सर्वसूत्रधारसुत: ॥

"In the Saṁvat year 1464 [A.D. 1407], mason Padumavi, son of the mason Sat." General Cunningham's reading *samapt* or *samâpt* is incorrect.

Inscription No. XVI is recorded in two lines on the second square pillar in the lower storey of the south-west cloister.

[1] सम्वत् १४६४

[2] बूनी चादी परी ॥

"In Saṁvat 1464 this building was finished."

Inscription No. XVII is engraved in two lines on the third pillar in the upper storey of the south-west cloister.

[1] समये

[2] सम्वत् १४६४ ॥

"In the Saṁvat year 1464."

Inscription No. XVIII is engraved in two lines on the second pillar in the upper storey of the north-west cloister.

[1] मङ्गलं महाश्री: ॥

[2] सम्वत् १४६५ चैत्रवदि ५ बुधे ॥

"[*May*] favourable fortune [*and*] great felicity [*attend*]! On Wednesday, the fifth day of the dark fortnight, in the month of Chaitra, in 1465 of the Saṁvat era," corresponding to Wednesday, the 23rd March 1408 A.D.

CHAPTER V.

KHÂLIS MUKHLIS AND JHANJHRÎ MASJIDS.

A work of the same reign and probably a few years earlier than the Ataladevî masjid is still undamaged, save by loss of any cloisters or gate it may have boasted. This is the masjid Dârîba, Khâlis Mukhlis, or Char angulî, built on the site of a favourite temple of Vijayachandra by Malik Khâlis and Malik Mukhlis, governors of Jaunpûr under Sulṭân Ibrâhîm, and described in one place as his chief nobles, in another as *chelas* of Fîrûz, but of whom one was at all events a namesake of the only one of Ibrâhîm's brothers, of whom a separate and important command is recorded. Vijayachandra is said to have prefaced his devotions in the temple erected by himself, by bathing in the *Khâs hauz*,—an enormous stone tank, three quarters of a mile from his palace, and still to be traced north of the great masjid,—and proceeding thence on foot to the temple. The masjid was erected for the convenience of Sa'îd Ûsmân, a reputed saint, born at Shirâz, driven from Dehlî by the irruption of Tîmûr; his descendants are said to dwell near the masjid which was rescued by Mr. Welland, a former Collector of Jaunpûr, from the desecrating occupancy of the neighbouring Korîs. It consists of a domed hall and two wings, the dome masked by a low façade of the character peculiar to Jaunpûr, but there is no ornament to break or relieve the sombre massiveness of the building. The name by which it is most commonly known is Char angulî, given it by reason of a stone in the south pier bearing a line three inches long, which should measure four fingers whosesoever be the hand measuring. Much *pûja* is done by Hindûs to this miraculous stone, and it is immensely revered by Musalmâns—even if they do not daub it with oil or pay any such outward respect.

Of the remaining building of this age nothing is left but the great piers, flanking a screen of such beauty as to show that the completed building could have been inferior in size only even to the famous Atala, the work of the same founder, and doubtless designed by the same architect (see Plate XXV). Wishing to build a masjid in honour of one Hazrat Sa'îd Sadr Jahân Ajmâlî, Ibrâhîm demolished the temple which Jayachandra had built at Muktaghâṭ, and on its site erected this building occupying part of the west side of a large court. Part of the court walls were knocked down by Sikandar Lodî, and the stones appropriated for other public and private buildings, and conspicuously for the great bridge. Floods in the ravine which it overhangs, and in the closely-adjoining Gûmtî, long since destroyed its vaults, and the brick enclosing-wall and low poor roof are the work of the last generation. Still, though it is kept clean and in order, the little court is more used for drying grain than as a place of prayer; for, though within the Sipâh mahallâh, it is a quarter of a mile from the city, and its nearest neighbours are the dead Pathâns whose tombs are in Châchakpûr. It is commonly known as the Jhanjhrî masjid, on account of the "screen-like" appearance of its ornamentation; and though very little known is well worthy of a visit, both on account of its past beauty and as showing now completely what in the Jaunpûr style seems an inner true arch is merely a part of the screen; for its voussoirs here—all carved with a long raised Arabic inscription (Nos. XIX and XX), the only instance in Jaunpûr of such a decoration—are all loose, and but for the support of the pierced screen would fall.

Inscription No. XIX is written in very fine Tughrâ characters round the two sides of the arch; the characters are 1′ 4″ long.

اَللّٰهُ لَا اِلٰهَ اِلَّا هُوَ الْحَيُّ الْقَيُّوْمُ لَاتَاخُذُهُ سِنَةٌ وَّلَا نَوْمٌ لَهُ مَا فِی السَّمٰوٰتِ وَمَا فِی الْاَرْضِ مَنْ ذَالَّذِي

يَشْفَعُ عِنْدَهُ اِلَّا بِاِذْنِهٖ يَعْلَمُ مَابَيْنَ اَيْدِيهِمْ وَمَا خَلْفَهُمْ وَلَا يُحِيطُوْنَ بِشَيْءٍ مِنْ عِلْمِهٖ اِلَّا بِمَا شَاءَ وَ سِعَ

كُرْسِيُّهُ السَّمٰوٰتِ وَالْاَرْضِ وَلَا يَؤُدُهُ حِفْظُهُمَا وَ هُوَ الْعَلِيُّ الْعَظِيمُ لَا اِكْرَاهَ فِی الدِّيْنِ قَدْ تَبَيَّنَ الرُّشْدُ مِنَ الْغَيِّ

فَمَنْ يَكْفُرْ بِالطَّاغُوتِ وَ يُوْمِنْ بِاللّٰهِ فَقَدِ اسْتَمْسَكَ بِالْعُرْوَةِ الْوُثْقٰى لَاانْفِصَامَ لَهَا وَاللّٰهُ سَمِيْعٌ عَلِيْمٌ

"Allah! there is no God but He, the living, the self-subsisting. Sleep and slumber do not overcome Him. Every heavenly and earthly thing belongs to Him. Who can intercede with Him except by His own permission? He knows their present and past, and His knowledge does not come within their compass. His throne extends over heaven and earth, and their preservation is not burdensome to Him. He is the high, the mighty. There is no hatred in the religion; certainly, guidance has been produced from depravity. He who retrograded from Satan and relied upon God, surely he professed the firm creed which cannot be broken, and God is the hearer and wise." [*Qurân*, Sûrah II.]

Inscription No. XX is engraved in Tughrâ characters on the base of the pointed arch.

قَالَ النَّبِيِّ صَلَّى اللّٰهُ عَلَيْهِ وَ سَلَّمْ مِنْ بَنَيَ لِلّٰهِ مَسْجِدًا يَبْتَغِي بِهٖ وَجْهِ اللّٰهِ بَنَي لَهُ بَيْتًا فِی

الْجَنَّةِ وَ قَالَ الرَّسُوْلَ اللّٰهِ صَلَّى اللّٰهُ عَلَيْهِ وَ اٰلِهٖ وَ سَلَّمْ مِنْ بَنَيَ مَسْجِدِ اللّٰهِ تَبَارَكَ وَ يَعْبُدُ فِيهِ اللّٰهِ

بَنَيَ اللّٰهِ لَهُ بَيْتًا فِی الْجَنَّةِ

"The Prophet—blessings upon him!—has said that 'who builds a masjid for God in hopes to countenance God, God builds a similar mansion for him in Paradise;' and the Prophet of God—blessings upon him!—has said that 'who builds a masjid in honour of God, and God is worshipped therein, God makes a mansion for him in Paradise.'" [*Hadis*].

CHAPTER VI.

LÂL DARWÂZA MASJID.

The sole remaining work of Mahmûd's reign is the masjid known as the Lâl Darwâza, so called in memory of the "high gate painted with vermilion" belonging to the palace which Bîbî Râjî built at the same time close by. It is the smallest of the masjids at Jaunpûr and stands at some distance to the north-west of the city. The style of the architecture is the same as that of the Jâmi and Atala masjids, but in them the Hindû type is less strongly visible than in this. The main walls are not so thick, and the edifice throughout is on a much lighter and less massive scale.

It is constructed of stone and brick with cement, but principally of stone. Externally as well as internally, all the walls are of ashlar masonry neatly tooled, with fine joints which are so beautifully worked that in thickness they hardly exceed that of the blade of a knife. Unfortunately this does not apply to the portion recently "restored," which is very inferior in every respect to the older work. The bricks used are very small and thin: in some places they run eight or nine courses to the foot, inclusive of joints. They vary in length, some being 4½ and others 3 inches long, and are used principally as a backing to the ashlaring of the walls. Throughout the building the columns and shafts are of stone, and each of those on the outer face of the cloisters fronting the piazza or courtyard is of one piece. The dome, roofs, copings, &c., are floated with cement on their external faces. The courtyard is not paved, differing in this respect from the other masjids, but the paving may have been removed.

The building generally is in a sadly dilapidated state, and should if possible be repaired. Portions have indeed been so treated, but in such bad form that one almost wishes such restoration had not been attempted. Such work should clearly be conducted only by officers who have received a special training in architecture. If a building cannot be restored properly, it is perhaps best left alone, with only just the necessary repairs done to it to prevent its falling altogether.

How this fabric escaped untouched when Sikandar Lodî destroyed the palace, it is hard to say. From the evidence of the stones lying about, which have fallen in the lapse of time, it is evident that the stones of this, like all the other masjids of Jaunpûr, had before been used in Hindû or Buddhist buildings. Churchwardens are the same all the world over, and though at the hours of prayer only a few stragglers push open the heavy gate to enter and pay their devotions, the mellowed stone-work of the masjid was not long ago treated to a liberal coat of whitewash (see Plate XXVII), though the courtyard and cloister roofs were not freed from the rank jangal grass. There is nothing very peculiar about the plan: three gates give access to a large court, with a cloister of one storey only running round, on the west side of which stands the masjid, the wings double the height of the cloister, the dome of the central hall masked as usual by a propylon (see Plate XXVI). The pendentives of the dome and the flat roof of the wings rest immediately on slender pillars, and there is nothing resembling an upper floor anywhere, save that on each side of the central hall is a raised gallery for women, approached by a stair formed in the piers of the propylon.

The date of erection, or any allusion to the founder, is nowhere inscribed, though in two places within are passages from the *Qurán* (Inscriptions XXI and XXII), and high on the screen without is a black stone bearing the *Kalimah*, or Musalmân confession of faith. On the whole this is the least interesting, though most perfect, of the great Moghal buildings at Jaunpûr.

The general arrangement of the plan (Plate XXVIII) resembles that of the A t a l a and J â m i masjids, but on a smaller scale. As it *now* stands it measures 190′ 0″ from east to west and 171′ 0″ from north to south, but were the shops extant these dimensions would be increased to 200′ 0″ and 186′ 0″ respectively.

On the north, south, and east sides are massive entrance gateways, through which access is gained to courtyard, cloisters, and masjid proper (Plate XXVI), which stands on the western side. The cloisters are only two bays deep, whilst those at the A t a l a are three. On the external walls of the cloisters are remains of square pilasters, from which we gather that originally a row of shops surrounded the masjid on the north, south, and east sides.

The masjid proper measures 168′ 6″ by 35′ 4″ inside dimensions, and is divided into three portions—a central chamber and an oblong room on either side—four aisles in depth, having five openings to the courtyard and two into the north and south cloisters. The central apartment over which stands a dome—the only one in the masjid—is square in plan and measures 22′ 7½″ each way; in front of it is an entrance hall three bays in width, a feature which does not exist in the other masjids.

In the north-west angle of the courtyard a room has been formed by building lateral walls across the cloisters, but inasmuch as on examining the masonry we found it constituted no part of the original design, it is only dotted in on the plan.

In the entrance gateways on the north, south, and east façades are staircases which at one time afforded access to the roofs over the cloisters and shops. The cloisters are only one storey, high, whilst those of the A t a l a are two storeys, with the exception of the mezzanine floors introduced on the right and left sides of the central chamber under the dome, and which were doubtless used as *zanána* courts.

The propylon (Plates XXVI and XXIX), the principal feature of the fabric, is 48′ 6″ high from the floor of the entrance hall and 44′ 9″ wide at the base, whilst the breadth across the top is but 43′ 0″, showing the usual diminution or batter found in other examples of this style of architecture. The towers contain staircases leading to the loft or mezzanine floor and the top of the propylon—whence the hours of prayer were announced, and which thus served the place of minarets.

Their façades are broken up and divided into storeys by means of deep horizontal and highly-decorated string-courses or table-mouldings. In the centre of the second, third, and fourth storeys are introduced ornamented arched recesses or niches, which measure 5′ 0″ by 3′ 0″ and are recessed some 1′ 6″ from the main face of the masonry. The arches are cusped and stand on octagonal shafts; in the tympanum of each is carved a lotus rosette, and below this runs a horizontal band forming an inner panel which is similarly treated, but instead of the rosette the bell ornament is seen hanging from the crown of the arch. In the spandrils of the arches small rosettes are carved.

The top of the propylon is crowned by an elaborate and bold cornice with a frieze, below which the surface is divided into panels filled in with cusped arches and decorated with small rosettes. The space between the bottom of the frieze and the fourth string-course is relieved by a square panel containing a very peculiar geometrical device that resembles a seven-pointed star, enclosing a circle and surrounded by a larger one. The same device is also carved over the principal *mihrâb* under the dome (see Plates XXVII and XXIX, Fig. 1). The great arch between the towers is of a double "ogee" form made up of two portions (one projecting in front of the other) and carried on moulded corbels: it is slightly stilted. The space under the arch is filled in with a stone screen pierced by three openings, the trellis-work of which has disappeared, and through this the exterior of the dome is visible. Over the central opening the *Kalimah* or Musalmân creed is engraved in large letters on black stone. The screen is carried on massive stone lintels which rest on large bracket capitals springing from the heads of the piers of the entrance hall or vestibule that leads to the area under the dome.

In the spandrils above the arch double rosettes are carved.[1] To the right and left of the propylon are the colonnades of the masjid proper. These are one storey in height, with the exception of the first two bays on each side, which have been divided into two low storeys, the upper one having been provided for the ladies of the court, who could thence witness and listen to the religious ceremonies carried on below. All the columns are square, and those forming the outer row are coupled. They are made up of two shafts placed one on the top of the other and surmounted by triple capitals.[2] The space between the columns is spanned by stone beams upon which the superstructure is carried. The wooden railing round the mezzanine floor or loft forms no part of the original design, but occupies the place of a former elaborate stone screen of which portions still remain on the sides looking into the dome.

The respective positions of dome and propylon are seen in the south elevation, Plate XXIX, Fig. 2. The dome stands considerably back from the rear of the propylon, and in this respect differs from that of the Atala masjid which impinges upon it. This is accounted for by the introduction of the vestibule below, which does not exist in the other masjids. The drum is octagonal, and in each of its sides is placed a trellis window to admit light. Of this the details are given on Plate XXXVII, Figs. 1, 2, 3. Over the angles above the string-course are polygonal finials (see Plate XXXVII, Fig. 4), and between these run two broad plainly-ornamanted encircling frieze bands (see Plate XL, Fig. 1), from the top of which spring flat ribs dividing the outer surface of the dome into panels. The top of the dome is crowned by an elaborate finial standing on a large inverted shell-like base.

The arched recesses shown on the outer wall of the masjid proper were originally entrances to the colonnade, but in the recent restoration they have been filled in. The southern gateway is a reproduction of that standing on the north side of the courtyard (Plate XXXII). The whole of the façade is in a most deplorable and dilapidated condition, and, but for the two or three piers remaining on either side of this and the east entrance, no one would imagine that shops ever existed on the outer face of the courtyard.

[1] For a general view of the propylon see Plate XXVI.

[2] For detail see Plate XL, Fig. 2.

The main features of the west façade (Plate XXX, Fig. 1) remind one of the Atala and Jâmi masjids. It is simple, yet majestic, and the grouping of the masses most effective. Between the flanking turrets or bastions at either end it measures 173′ 4″, and stands nearly 26′ 0″ high from the ground-level. The massiveness of the masonry is relieved by the bold horizontal string-courses which, like the plinth, run the entire length of the façade and terminate on the end walls of the masjid proper. The central portion in front of the dome projects from the main wall and is strengthened by pinnacle-capped bastions—counterparts of those standing at the angles of the fabric. The openings on either side light the mezzanine floor (Plate XXXI). At the back of the propylon are the steps leading to its summit. With the exception of the cornice running round the top, none of the elaborate decoration of the front and sides is repeated here.

The central chamber of the masjid proper is square in plan and covered by a dome 22′ 8″ in diameter which rests on an octagonal frame-work of massive stone lintels stretching from column to column, the angles of which are cut off and a sixteen-sided figure developed upon which the cupola of the dome is supported (see Plate XXX, Fig. 2). The sides forming the drum are panelled, arched, and filled in with stone trellis-work; eight are pierced to admit light to the upper part of the chamber (see Plate XXXVII, Fig. 1). The total height from the floor-level to the crown measures 41′ 4½″. The only piece of furniture in the entire masjid is the *mimbár* or pulpit which projects from the west wall. Passing through the entrance hall or vestibule we enter the piazza or courtyard and have a full view of the northern cloister. It is a one-storey building, only 8′ 4″ high to the underside of the lintels and two aisles deep; the columns of the inner row are octagonal and those of the outer row square (see Plate XXXIX). The rear wall is panelled in the centre of each bay, for detail of which see Plate XXXIV, Figs. 4, 5. The section cuts through the eastern gateway and shows the difference in height between the chamber in front and the cloisters on each side. The columns of this chamber—which is oblong in plan—are of one height, square and single, with the exception of the outer row on each side, which are coupled. On each side of the entrance is a staircase leading to the top of the gateway and the roof over the cloister.

On the north and south sides of the dome the only double storey in the entire building has been introduced (Plates XXVIII and XXXI). It was constructed for the use of the ladies of the court for devotional purposes. Access to it is gained by the staircases in the tower of the propylon. The sides looking into the dome and colonnades are filled in with stone trellis-work of a pretty design. The west wall is divided into bays, two of which serve as *mihrábs*, whilst the third is utilized to admit light. The *mihrábs* are recessed 1′ 2″ from the face of the wall and encased by broad, flat, richly-carved architraves (Fig. 5). At the corners of the recess, angle shafts (Fig. 4) support the arches above, in the spandrils of which are carved small rosettes. In the tympanum beneath, a large rosette is introduced, whilst below the field of the panel is relieved by the bell ornament.

The north gateway (Plate XXXII) and the entrance on the south are the counterparts of each other. In general design they resemble the large propylon, except that they stand on a heavy-panelled plinth. Like the propylon the gateway tapers upwards, measuring across the base 22′ 4″, but at the top only 21′ 0″, with a total height of 21′ 0″, the block forming almost a square and presenting a solid and somewhat massive Doric or

Egyptian-like appearance. The flight of steps leading from the road-level to the courtyard has crumbled away, and portions remain only here and there to indicate its former existence at all.

The heavy appearance of the tower on each side of the entrance is relieved by niches or recesses and ornamental string-courses similar in design to those employed in the decoration of the large propylon. The arch between the towers rests on moulded stone corbels, and the masonry of the tympanum is carried on lintels spanning the entrance. The spandrils over the outer ring of the arch are set back some 4" from the face of the masonry of the towers, and are enriched by a deep bead running round the three sides and by the introduction of large rosettes.

The abrupt termination of the top is perhaps hardly pleasing; a cornice seems wanting; but for some reason the architect did not supply it. It may be thought by some that such originally existed, but this can hardly have been so, as the north and south entrances of the Atala masjid are treated in a similar way.

Of the three entrances to the masjid the eastern or main gateway (Plate XXXIII) is the largest and most important. It stands 30′ 0″ high from the topmost step of the flight leading up from the road, and measures across the base 25′ 4″. The sides taper towards the top, which measures only 24′ 3″. Like the entrances on the north and south sides, it stands on a massive panelled pedestal. The tower on either side is broken up by highly-decorated string-courses and deeply-recessed niches of the same design as those of the north entrance. But the main arch is treated differently, inasmuch as the soffit is cusped and the screen wall under it divided into large panels set in flat and decorated borders, the centre one of which originally contained an inscription, while those on each side and the spandrils of the arch are ornamented with carved rosettes.

The spandrils over the main arch are set back and enriched by diaper work of a plain and effective design, over which runs a floral frieze. The top of the entrance is crowned by a cornice, the principal feature of which is a bold torus moulding supported by a carved corona or band slightly projecting from the face of the wall.

The principal *mihrāb* (Plate XXXIV, Figs. 1, 2, 3) is always placed in the centre of the internal face of the west wall of the masjid proper—looking towards Makka. Of all the *mihrābs* in this fabric it is the finest, and standing as it does immediately in front of the principal entrance, is seen directly the chamber under the dome is entered. In plan it is oblong, supported by angle shafts composed of small turned balusters and cable or twisted pillars separated by carved dies, from the tops of which spring ornamented cusped arches. The background is panelled, and carved on the face is the bell ornament. The soffit of the *mihrāb* is domed over and divided into panels by moulded ribs. The spandrils over the outer arch are panelled and ornamented with *pateræ*. The whole is encased by a flat architrave projecting slightly from the wall. In the Atala masjid this is beautifully carved, but not so here.

Plate XXXIV, Fig. 4, shows the system of panelling prevalent in the cloister walls of this and the other masjids at Jaunpûr. In this example they are recessed some 8″ from the face of the wall, and each measures 6′ 6″ high by 2′ 9″ broad. They are divided into three compartments by horizontal bands in continuation of the masonry courses, the topmost being arched over and the spandril above panelled.

Fig. 5 is a cross section through the cloisters which surround the piazza or courtyard on the north, south, and east sides. These are two aisles in depth and contain two rows of columns, the outer of which is square and the inner octagonal. The roof is constructed of stone and brick with cement on the usual Indian principles. Stone beams cross from cap to cap of the columns, and upon the square frame-work thus formed other beams of the same material run at right angles over which the intervening space is filled in. Upon this is placed concrete and the whole floated over with a thick coat of cement.

On reference to the ground plan (Plate XXVIII and elevation on Plate XXIX, Fig. 1) the positions of the recesses shown in Plate XXXV will be seen. In plan they are square and set back 1′ 4″ from the main face of the wall. The backs are panelled, arched, and decorated with the usual bell and *patera*. At the inner angles stand shafts made up of small turned balusters and ornamented dies. Over the front of each is turned a cusped arch the spandrils of which are panelled and carved with rosettes.

These small panels (Plate XXXVI), 1′ 8½″ by 2′ 0½″, stand immediately over the recesses referred to on Plate XXXV. They are slightly sunk from the face of the wall, and are of the same design as the inner panels of the *mihrâbs* below.

In Plate XXXVII, Figs. 1, 2, and 3, are given a detail of the windows which pierce the drum of the dome. In plan they are square with deep reveals. The inner openings are filled in with stone trellis-work of a varied design—a characteristic of this style of architecture.

The finials on the exterior of the dome (Plate XXXVII, Fig. 4) stand at the angles of the octagon forming the drum. In design they resemble some of the columns in the cloisters below. The lower portion is octagonal, the centre sixteen-sided, and the upper round and surmounted by a cap.

Plate XXXVII, Fig. 5, gives a detail of the cornice round the interior of the dome over the large pier supporting the drum.

The panel over the principal *mihrâb* under the dome (Plate XXXVIII) is square, 2′ 10½″ by 2 10½″, and projects slightly from the face of the wall. The design, which is peculiar, is likewise introduced in the upper part of the propylon (see Plates XXVI and XXIX, Fig. 1). The centre is slightly concave and surrounded by a plain, flat, circular band: around this is a heptagonal figure, the seven sides of which form bases for as many triangles of white stone standing on a black ground and encompassed by a circle resting on a square. The whole is set in a frame, the sides of which are ornamented by a continuous, repeating, floral scroll.

Plate XXXIX, Fig. 1, represents one of the inner row of columns of the cloister on the south side. The lower portion of the column is octagonal, the central sixteen-sided, and the upper cylindrical, tapered and fluted at the top. The cap is round and slightly moulded at the top and bottom.

Fig. 2 is an example of the outer row of piers to the cloisters, and which throughout the masjid are square. It is most crude, and were it not for the moulded caps and bracket corbels or sur-capital supporting the stone beams above, would savour little of architectural treatment.

Figs. 3 and 4 are examples of some of the older columns standing in the west cloister. Fig. 3 is somewhat similar to Fig. 1, but differs in these respects: the rounded cap is converted into one of sixteen sides; the cylindrical portion of the shaft is neither so long nor tapered nor fluted, but is broken up by a slightly projecting octagonal band;

and the lower octagonal portion is made longer. Fig. 4 is brought within the domain of architecture by cutting off the angles a foot below the neck, and enriching with lotus ornamentation, &c., &c., four out of the eight sides thus formed. A detail of one side is given in fig. 5. The base of the shaft is also profusely carved, but in a rather inferior style.

The whole of the bases, columns, caps and bracket capitals are of stone, each of the shafts being in one solid piece.

All the above are typical of Indian architecture and tend to support the theory that both this and the other masjids at Jaunpûr are largely constructed of materials which originally formed part of Buddhist or Hindû temples destroyed by the Muhammadans and afterwards used by them in the erection of their masjids.

From the top of the band to the underside of the string-course round the exterior of the dome (Plate XL, fig. 1) measures 5′ 2″, out of which the string itself is only 9″ deep. It projects from the face of the wall 3¼″ and is made up of plain chamfered mouldings. The lower band springs from the top of the string-course and stands some 7¾″ in advance of the upper one. The tops of both are embattled and incised by deeply cut crosses. The angles of the dome are emphasized by finials of similar design to the columns in the cloisters below. The caps remain on a few only (Plate XXX, fig. 1), most of them having been destroyed by time.

The capitals surmounting the shafts forming the one-storied colonnade on each side of the dome in the masjid (Plate XXIX, fig. 1, and detail of Plate XL, fig. 2) are made up of three distinct and separate parts, a lower, middle, and upper, the combined height being 3′ 9.″ The lower is of one piece of stone, and is plainly moulded. The abacus is chamfered at the top, and the face ornamented with raised floral carving. The cymatium is composed of two broad fillets, from the upper of which hang pointed facets, the lower is chamfered and projects slightly over the neck which is composed of three narrow bands below which projects a double splayed necking supported on the underside by two small overlapping fillets. The middle consists of four bell corbels, one on each of the sides of the pier, with hooded facet caps and broad bands over, upon which stand the large bracket capitals supporting the architraves or stone beams that carry the roof above.

The shaft is made up of two pieces of stone connected by a broad projecting band, bevelled at the top, and roughly moulded at the bottom. The bases to this and all the other columns throughout the masjid proper are perfectly plain.

Inscriptions.

The following inscriptions have been found in the Lâl Darwâza Masjid.

Inscription No. XXI is written in Arabic characters on the top of the outer frame of the central *mihráb.*

قوله تعالى إنّ الله وملائكته يصلّون على النبيّ يا ايها الذين آمنوا صلّوا عليه وسلّموا تسليما

"God has said :—'Surely, God and His angels bless the Prophet; ye believers bless Him, and offer peace and benediction.'" [*Qurán.*]

Inscription No. XXII is written in fine Tughrâ characters on the two sides of the inner pointed arch.

اللّٰهُ لَا اِلٰهَ اِلَّا هُوَ الْحَيُّ الْقَيُّومُ لَا تَاْخُذُهُ سِنَةٌ وَّلَا نَوْمٌ لَهُ مَا فِى السَّمٰوٰتِ وَمَا فِى الْاَرْضِ مَنْ

ذَالَّذِي يَشْفَعُ عِنْدَهُ اِلَّا بِاِذْنِهِ يَعْلَمُ مَا بَيْنَ اَيْدِيهِمْ وَمَا خَلْفَهُمْ وَلَا يُحِيطُونَ بِشَيْءٍ مِنْ عِلْمِهِ اِلَّا بِمَا شَاءَ وَسِعَ

كُرْسِيُّهُ السَّمٰوٰتِ وَالْاَرْضَ وَلَا يَؤُدُهُ حِفْظُهُمَا وَهُوَ الْعَلِيُّ الْعَظِيمُ

"God! there is no God but He who is living and self-subsisting. Sleep and slumber do not seize Him. Every heavenly and earthly thing belongs to Him. None can intercede with Him save His own permission. He knows their present and past, and His knowledge does not come within their compass except what He pleases. His throne extends over heaven and earth and their preservation is not burdensome to Him. He is the high, the mighty." [*Qurân*, Sûrah II.]

Inscription No. XXIII is carved on the third pillar of the middle row of the north-east corner of the cloisters. "Saṁvat 1128," A.D. 1071, is only readable, whilst the few letters of five different lines, still visible on a narrow strip, are too indistinct, the rest of the original flat surface having been cut away to form a round shaft. The original stone is now in the Lucknow Provincial Museum, as the shaft fell down some years ago, broke, and was replaced by a new square pillar.

Inscription No. XXIV is cut in two lines on the face of the bracket-capital of the fourth square pillar, first row, in the south-east cloister. The two lines are both incomplete on the right hand, owing to the cutting away of three and a half inches of the face to make the old Hindû bracket fit into its new position in the Muhammadan masjid. As both the date and the last letters of the name are in perfect order, it is possible to complete the missing part with absolute certainty. The date of the inscription shows that it belongs to the time of Vijayachandra Dêva of Kanauj; these few letters just occupy three and a half inches of space which was cut away.

[1] संवत् १२२५ चैत्रवदि ५ बुधे श्री [मद्विजयच-]

[2] न्द्रदेवराज्ये भट्टारकश्रीभुविभूष[णः॥]

"In the Saṁvat year 1225 (A.D. 1168), on the 5th day of the dark fortnight of the month Chaitra, on Wednesday,[1] during the reign of the fortunate Vijayachandra Dêva, the venerable Bhuvibhûshaṇa."

The term *bhaṭṭâraka* signifies either a *muni* or a Buddhist teacher. Bhuvibhûshaṇa is therefore the name of a Brâhmaṇ or a Buddhist who, in A. D. 1168, paid his devotions at the temple from where the bracket was brought. The *Vijayamandiram*, or the temple of Vijayachandra Dêva, stood in this quarter of the city, and it seems probable that many pillars and stones of the Lâl Darwâza masjid were brought from such a convenient quarry.

Inscription No. XXV is recorded in eleven lines on two faces of the fourth octagonal pillar, middle row, of the south-west cloister. It gives a long list of Hindû pilgrims, both males and females, who visited, on Thursday, the first day of the waning moon of Chaitra, in the Saṁvat year 1297, probably the temple of Vijayachandra Dêva from

[1] Corresponding to Wednesday, the 27th March 1168 A.D.

whence this pillar was brought. The date corresponds to Thursday, the 21st March 1240. On the second face of the octagonal pillar, only a few characters are visible. The names of the pilgrims are written in very large nail-shaped Devanâgarî letters.

Inscription No. XXVI is cut in ten lines on two faces of the third octagonal pillar first row, of the north-west cloister. The date Saṁvat 1353 is, besides, confirmed by the addition of the corresponding year, *Plava*, of the *Bṛihaspati chakra*, or sixty-year cycle of Jupiter, which by the reckoning used in Northern India was Saṁvat 1353.

[1] ओं नमो गणपतये ॥ अयोध्यायां
[2] पुरा वृत्तः सत्यवाक्सुजनप्रियः [।] स-
[3] ढेसाधुरिति ख्यातः सर्व्वसत्वहिते रतः [॥१॥]
[4] तस्य पुत्रो बभूवाथ साधुनिधेति विश्रु-
[5] तः [।] तस्यात्मजः शुचिर्धीरः पद्मसाधुरयं
[6] भुवि ॥ [२॥] काश्यां विश्वेश्वरद्वारि हिमाद्रिशि
[7] [1]खरोपमम् । पद्मेश्वरस्य देवस्य प्रासाद-
[8] मकरोत्सुधीः ॥ [३॥] ज्येष्ठे मासि सिते पक्षे
[9] द्वादश्यां बुधवासरे [।] लिखितेयं सदा
[10] याति प्रशस्तिः प्लववत्सरे ॥ [४॥] संवत् १३५३ [॥]

"Oṁ! glory be to Gaṇapati (Gaṇeśa)! In Ayodhyâ[2] lived formerly Saḍhesâdhu, the speaker of truth, the beloved of good men, whose delight consisted in the welfare of all beings. His son was the famous Sâdhunidhi, whose son, Padmasâdhu, of steadfast virtue, on the north side of the entrance to the Viśvêśvara temple at Kâśî built a solid and lofty temple of the god Padmêśvara (Vishṇu), on Wednesday, the twelfth day of the waning moon of the month of Jyaishṭha, in the year Plava : Saṁvat 1353, on which day this eulogy was written."

The date corresponds to Wednesday, the 15th May 1296 A.D. This important inscription shows clearly that this very pillar, and undoubtedly many others, were brought from Banâras. Below this inscription is twice recorded "Saṁvat 1504," or A.D. 1447, which most probably records the date of the erection of the cloisters.

Inscription No. XXVII is recorded on the face of the fifth octagonal pillar, middle row, of the north west cloister.

[1] विसद्रुसुत [:] कमऊ
[2] मिस्त्री [॥]

"Visadru's son, Kamaû, the architect." This simple record of the architect or head mason Kamaû is the most valuable inscription of the Lâl Darwâza, as it is another proof of the truth of Fergusson's remark, that the cause of the admixture of Hindû and Muhammadan styles in the Jaunpur masjids was the employment of Hindû masons.

[1] *Read* खरोपमं ।

[2] See *ante*, p. 9, note 3.

CHAPTER VII.

JÂMI MASJID.

Last among the buildings of Jaunpûr which require description is the splendid masjid of Husain Sharqî—the Jâmi Masjid. Of the reason for its foundation divers accounts are given, and some attribute the design to Ibrâhim, who wished to save an old hermit, Hazrat Khwâja Îsa, the voluntary labour of walking barefooted from his dwelling hard by to the Masjid Khâlis Mukhlis, a mile distant, for the Friday prayers. Others say that when during a seven-years' famine Husain found his overseers diverting to their own use the funds and supplies he had granted for the distressed, he devised a labour test, directing that only those should receive anything who laboured in casting up the mound which is now the court-yard of the masjid, and which stands some 16′ to 20′ above the road-level.

There is possibly truth in both stories. No one attributes any part of the building to Ibrâhim, but some such design may have occurred to him, for all his family lie in a cloistered court of a building close adjoining the north side of the masjid, probably round the grave of this Khwâja Îsa, who was certainly buried where he lived; the sanctity which made him a tempting grave-mate was enough to suggest the building a masjid in his honour. The famine, however, may have been invented to account for the raised court-yard, which surely needed no such explanation. Yet, be this as it may, the work must have occupied many years of Husain's reign, though it was not ready for dedication till after his fall. We may wonder that Bahlol allowed his fallen foe to complete and reap the credit of so magnificent a structure, and indeed even that Sikandar, in his rage at Husain's persistent treachery, was content with throwing down the eastern gate and somewhat damaging the cloisters, after vowing that not a stone should be left to record the existence of his rival.

The foundation of the Jâmi masjid was laid in A. H. 842, or A. D. 1438, "but it was not raised above the level of the ground in 844, when the king died," as Khair-ad-dîn states. It is said that the date of the completion of the masjid was found in the words *masjid Jámi us sharq*, which were engraved on the front of the eastern gate. This would fix the date in A. H. 852, or 1448 A. D., during the reign of Mahmûd Shâh Sharqî. But Khair-ad-dîn says that the work was at a standstill during the reign of Mahmûd Shâh, and was finished by Husain Shâh. Accordingly some people say the inscription on the eastern gate was *Al masjid Jámi us sharq*, which would make the date A. H. 883, or 1478 A. D. Khair-ad-dîn objects to this date, on the ground that the rule of the Sharqî kings had ceased; but Husain Shah's final defeat and abandonment of Jaunpûr did not take place until 884 A. H., as Khair-ad-dîn himself states in another place.

On a site sloping slightly southwards is a raised terrace some 16 to 20 feet high on the south, upon which the masjid is erected. The lower portion is almost on a level with the road, and on the north, south, and east sides (Plate XLVI) consists of a low range of small shops, in front of which is a veranda 9′ 7″ in width, and over them is an upper cloister. The west side is occupied by the lower portion of the masjid proper (Plates XLVII, LI, and LII). The court-yard (Plate LI, fig. 2) is surrounded on the north, south, and east sides by cloisters two aisles in depth, and now only one storey high, the second having been pulled down by Sikandar Lodî. In each of these sides is a massive domed entrance gateway approached by a steep flight of steps from below (see Plates XLVII, L, LI, and LXXII). The west side is occupied by the masjid proper and measures 59′ in depth by 235′ in length, including the thickness of the walls, but not the bastions at the angles. It is divided into five areas, a central room, 39′ 7½″ by 39′ 8½″ and roofed by a dome, a low-pillared room on each side 25′ 4″ by 44′ 7″, over which is the *zanâna* gallery (Plate XLVIII), and on each side of this again a lofty arched chamber 49′ 3″ in length by 39′ 7″ in width. These apartments are all connected by arched openings (see Plate LI, fig. 1).

The entire length of the inner face of the west wall is divided into bays by pilasters, and in the middle of each is a *mihrâb* (Plates LI, fig. 1, LIX, and LXI), the central one in each chamber being more ornate than the others.

The *zanâna* chapels are reached by staircases inside the piers of the propylons standing in front of the dome. In plan the galleries are oblong and divided into bays, six in length by three in breadth, by square stone columns (Plate LXII, fig. 3), the capitals over which support horizontal architraves dividing the ceiling into a series of panels, most of which are beautifully carved in low relief (Plates LXV and LXVI). The west wall is ornamented with *mihrâbs*, the details of which are given on Plates LXIII, and LXIV—the former illustrating that in the south chapel and the latter that in the north one. In plan and general design they are very much alike. The distinguishing feature is the difference between the architraves, the carving on that surrounding the *mihrâb* in the south chapel being of a totally different character from that enclosing the *mihrâb* in the north one. Again the angles of the architraves in the former are chamfered and ornamented with facets, whereas those of the latter are square and channelled on each side of the field of carving. The inner portion of the *mihrâbs* is recessed some 1′ 8″ from the face of the wall and is arch-panelled and cusped, and from the crown of the arch hangs the lamp ornament. The width across the inner portion of the *mihrâb* is 1′ 9″, whilst across the outer face, between the architraves, it measures 4′ 11″. The difference in dimensions is made up by inserting a connecting tier of angle shafts composed of small octagonal balusters and ornamented square dies, over the tops of which cusped arches are turned. The spandrils between the architraves and the extrados of the arch are panelled, moulded, and decorated with rosettes. The face of the tympanum of the inner arch is relieved by a boldly carved *patera*.

The section through the court-yard (Plate LI, fig. 2) shows the east entrance, which is in the same dismantled condition as it was left by Sikandar Lodî, and not, as asserted by some, "thrown down by Englishmen in order to repair the station roads." In the centre of the cloisters surrounding the quadrangle on the north and south sides are domed entrance gateways, both of which have recently been repaired. The cloisters are now only one storey in height. The pillars of which they are formed are all square, and most of them plain (Plate LXII, figs. 1,2), and probably were brought from the old Hindû fanes, which at one time existed in the immediate vicinity, as may perhaps be inferred from the mason's marks engraved thereon (Plate XLII).

The vaulted chamber at the south-west angle of the masjid is given in the transverse section (Plate LI, fig. 1). In length it is 49′ 3″ and in breadth 39′ 7½″. It is roofed in stone, and "the vault is so constructed that its upper surface forms the external roof of the building, which in Gothic vaults is scarcely ever the case."[1] In height the chamber is 44′ 4¼″ to the underside of the ridge. The internal face of the south wall is broken up by arched recesses, window openings, and ornamented string mouldings. The wall is 7′ 5″ in thickness and contains a staircase leading to the roof of the vaulted apartment, a longitudinal section of which is given on Plate LI, fig. 1. The upper portion of the western wall is quite plain, but the lower part is devoted to *mihrâbs*, three in number, and which stand in the centre of the bays formed by piers projecting 1′ 6″ from the wall, and over which spring the ribs dividing the vault into three casements. The central *mihrâb* is the largest and most important. It is recessed within the wall 3′ 5″ and enclosed in broad, flat, sunk, and richly-carved architraves. On each side of the opening are angle shafts supporting arches which are cusped, and the spandrils of which are panelled and decorated with rosettes. The soffit of the *mihrâb* is domed and divided into panels by flat projecting ribs of black stone. On each side of the *mihrâb* is a panel 2′ 0′ by 2′ 3½″ (Plate LXVIII, Fig. 1), the borders of which are richly carved and enclose a moulded inner panel, the upper portion of which is arch-like, and cut in the face of it is a Greek cross. The corresponding panel in the northern vaulted chamber differs somewhat from this (Plate LXVIII, Fig. 2), inasmuch as the outer border is ornamented with a star pattern instead of floral carving. The space under the arch is unadorned, but to make up for it the spandrils are incised with Greek crosses.

The low-pillared apartment separating this chamber from the dome is 13′ 4¼″ high and is divided into bays by square annuleted pillars surmounted by bracket capitals carrying stone lintels which support the ceiling and divide it into a series of panels, none of which are ornamented. The west wall is occupied by *mihrâbs*.

The central chamber of the masjid proper is square in plan, and is certainly the most imposing and ornate feature of the fabric. The walls on the north, south, and east sides are pierced by arched openings, and the west wall is recessed with elaborate *mihrâbs* (Plate LIX). Just above the arched openings the square form of the room changes into that of an octagonal figure, and which is superseded by one of sixteen sides supporting a stone cupola by which the chamber is roofed. In design the apartment resembles that of the Atala Masjid, but of the two that is more chaste and refined in detail. The internal height of the room is 67′ 6″. According to Kittoe, "the dome is a wonderful piece of workmanship, the exterior shell being many feet apart from that of the interior, and is formed by different segments of circles;" and Major-General Cunningham[2] informs us there must be some arrangement of this kind, as by his measurement the top of the dome outside is 67′ 3″, whilst the inside is only 55′ 3″, shewing a difference of 12 feet, and as this is too much for the top thickness of a single dome, he concludes there are two thin domes, each about 3′ 0′ in thickness at the top, and thus leaving an empty space of 6 feet in height. But the true height of the dome on the *inside* is 67′ 6″ and not 55′ 3″, and outside the height is 72′ 6″ to the top of the cap which supports the finial. The thickness of the wall, measured through the window openings

[1] Fergusson's *Indian and Eastern Architecture*, p. 523.
[2] *Archæological Reports*, Vol. XI, p. 115.

in the drum of the dome also (Plate LI, fig. 1), is 3′ 0¾″, not 12′ 0″, and therefore could hardly support a double dome as above described; while at the vertex, including the cap, the whole thickness is only 5 feet. The diameter of the dome is 39′ 5″.

The beauty of the chamber impresses one directly it is beheld. Eight out of the sixteen sides in the upper storey—all of which are arched and enclosed in elaborate architraves—are pierced and filled in with baluster-like work, through which the light streams into the cupola, causing a rich play of light and shade over the whole extent of the chamber and produces a most charming picture. The remaining sides are filled in with screen-work, backed with masonry.

The octagonal sides of the drum are arched and the arch soffits cusped. They are enclosed in architraves richly carved, with a strap-work device; the spandrils are panelled, moulded, and ornamented with *pateræ*. The space under the arch is filled in with a pierced stone screen of eight panels (Plate LX) formed by mullions and transoms. The centre panel is open at the top, and in the lower portion is a flat balustrade. Through these screens the ladies of the *zanána* could witness the religious services conducted below. The *mihrábs* in the west wall below are three, the central one being the largest and most beautiful (Plate LIX). Between it and that on the north side stands the *mimbár* or pulpit. It is 6′ 0″ in height and 4′ 0″ in breadth. The *mihráb* measures 10′ 8″ across from out to out and is recessed in the wall 3′ 7″. On the external face is a flat architrave surrounding a chamfered jamb standing on a square plinth. On each side of the opening are three angle shafts of ornamented octagonal balusters and carved square dies, and over them cusped arches are turned. The soffit of the recess is canopied and panelled by projecting splayed ribs of black stone. A border of black stone encloses the inner panel, on which are engraved extracts from the *Qurán*. The spandrils over the arches are moulded and ornamented with *pateræ*, and over is a banderolle.

In front of the dome stands a majestic propylon 84′ 4″ high, in design somewhat similar to that of the Atala Masjid (see Plates XLIII and XLIX). It is larger, however, and more commanding, and constitutes a grand piece of architecture; and, standing as it does on a base raised some sixteen feet above the road-level, it towers over the adjoining buildings and becomes the most conspicuous object in the city. Across the base it measures 76′ 10½″, whilst across the top it is only 70′ 10″, shewing a slope in the walls of 3′ 0¼″ on each side. A lofty central arch 72′ 2″ in height connects these two massive piers which project some 10′ 0″ from the front of the main façade and contain stairs leading to the roof of the Masjid, and from thence to the top of the propylon. The piers are divided into five storeys by enriched horizontal string courses, and in the second, third, fourth, and fifth are elaborate arched niches, set in triple architraves. The spandrils over the main arch are ornamented with raised diaper work. The tympanum forms a screen to hide the dome, and is divided into two portions by elaborate bands of clustered mouldings. The lower part is pierced by six arched openings and the upper by nine, all of which, with the exception of the topmost, are arched and cusped and set in embellished architraves. The masonry on each side is carved with rosettes. The lower portion of the propylon is pierced by three entrances leading into the hall under the grand dome, and over them are as many windows lighting the corridor connecting the *zanána* gallery on the north with that on the south side of the Masjid. The propylon is now seen to a disadvantage, as unfortunately most of the splendid stone trellis-work with which the arched openings in the tympanum were filled is wanting. The central entrance (Plate LIII) leading from the front platform to the dome is bridged by a stone lintel resting on carved and moulded double bracket corbels, partly supported by moulded angle capitals. The soffit of the entrance (Plate LV) forms an elaborate and fine piece of panelled ceiling work. In the centre of a rhombus is an elaborate lotus *patera* encircled by a carved floral wreath, radiating and repeating in design. The masonry on each side of the entrance is divided into panels by broad bands of carving continued round the openings as architraves. In the side wall of the central entrance is an arched niche or recess (Plate LIV) standing over an enriched horizontal string-course. It is enclosed by a broad flat border of strap-work carving, portions of which are defaced. On each side are small baluster shafts. The back is panelled and relieved by lotus rosettes, which are unfortunately decayed, and, like the shafts, coated with whitewash. The spandrils are moulded, panelled, and ornamented with *patera*.

The detail of the niches ornamenting the massive piers of the propylon is given on Plate LVI. The inner portion consists of a perforated stone screen filled in at the back with ashlaring. It is recessed 1′ 3″ from the face of the wall, and is supported on each side by two angle shafts, from the tops of which four centred, stilted, and cusped arches spring. The niche is enclosed by triple architraves, the outer and inner jambs of which are raised 1½″ above the central one. Each is carved with a different design. In the tympanum and spandrils of the arch are rosettes.

The façade on each side of the propylon is pierced by arched openings, opposite to the *mihrâbs* in the west wall of the chambers within. The exterior of the long vaulted apartment is emphasised by a deep moulded string course, over which is a row of ornamented panels with a Greek cross cut in the spandrils over the inner arched panel. Both the north and south sides of the piers of the propylon are ornamented by four oblong recessed panels, and details of those in the southern pier are seen on Plates LVII, and LVIII. In design they are rich and varied, and no two are alike in their architraves.

The shafts, the screen work over the transoms, and the carved panels under the cusped arches all differ. Under each recess is a string moulding elaborately carved and returned on the west side of the propylon, which is plain in design, and pierced here and there by latticed window openings, lighting the steep stairs within. In the rear of the propylon stands the grand dome, the drum of which is octagonal. In the middle of each side stood kiosks, four of which still remain. The drum of the dome is crowned by a deep frieze, ornamented and carved (Plate LXX), and parts of it have been wrought into a design for which they were never intended. The base of the cupola is encircled by a band of arabesque incised ornament (Plate LXXI, fig. 1), executed in a kind of encaustic tile work in red and white pigments. Below is a narrow, hollow, chamfered table moulding. The cupolas of the kiosks are ornamented in a similar way (Plate LXXI, fig. 2). On each side of the dome is seen the roof over the vaulted chamber in the Masjid proper below, and like the cupola of the great dome and those over the north and south entrances to the quadrangle, is floated in cement, although the interior is of stone. The side elevation of the north and south entrance is shown on the west external façade (Plates XLIV and LII). In general design the western front resembles a fortified building. The walls are sloped to give an appearance of strength, and the angles are emphasized by bastions, which are divided into three tiers by heavy string courses (Plates LXV, LXVIII, LXIX), which continue the whole length of the façade and stop on the lateral walls of the Masjid.

Till near the end of 1887 a stone staircase stood at the north-west angle of the Masjid and afforded access to the northern *zanána* gallery. It was an essential part of the original structure, but was unfortunately removed by the local authorities on account of its supposed instability.

The north side of the fabric (Plate L) is in a dilapidated condition (not more so, however, than the eastern), more especially the north-east angle. The cloister on the west angle of the court-yard has lately been repaired. Beneath is a row of shops, and over these should be another storey, evidence of which remains in the pilasters and capitals at the north-east angle of the Masjid proper. The gate entrance to the quadrangle in the centre of the façade has been *restored* by the Muhammadan community, and unfortunately without regard to that on the south side of the quadrangle (Plate LXXII), which is very effective in design.

It is approached by a steep flight of stone steps extending the whole width of the gateway, which is 43′ 11½″ high, 37′ 10¼″ across the top, and 40′ across the base. It projects in front of the cloisters about 22′. The central part is recessed some 5′ and spanned by a four-centred and slightly stilted arch. The spandrils over it are panelled, moulded, and ornamented with *pateræ*. The tympanum is unadorned and pierced by one small arched opening. The solid masonry on each side of the entrance is broken up by decorated string mouldings, and in the stories thus formed are arched recesses, the backgrounds of which are ornamented with richly-carved panels. The arches of the recesses are cusped and rest on angle shafts composed of two small octagonal balusters and three dies; the centre one is carved. In the rear is a square chamber which is roofed by a dome resting on an octagonal drum. It is counterpart to that on the north side of the quadrangle, a section of which is given on Plate LXXIII.

Like the Atala and Lál Darwâza Masjids, the edifice is constructed of ashlar stone masonry neatly tooled with fine joints. The domes, the roofs, the copings, &c., are floated in cement on the external faces.

The eastern half of the court-yard is covered with grass and trees, whilst the other is flagged and constitutes the praying place, on which the followers of Islâm congregate to perform their devotions.

Inscriptions.

The following inscriptions have been found in the Jâmi Masjid :—

Inscription No. XXVIII is written in fine Tughrâ characters on the top of the *mihráb* in the central hall.

بسم الله الرحمن الرحيم محمد رسول الله والذين اشداء على الكفار رحمك بينهم ترئهم ركعا

و سجدا يبتغون فضلا من الله و رضوانا سيماهم في وجوه هم اثر من السجود

"In the name of God, the merciful, the clement! Muhammad, the Prophet of God, and his companions, are mighty over the heathens. Among them you will find

1

people kneeling and bowing down. They gain favour and pleasure of God, and are discerned by the mark of adoration on their foreheads." [*Qurán*, Sûrah Faṭh.]

Inscription No. XXIX is written in Arabic characters round the outer margin of the pointed arch of the *mihráb* in the central hall.

اَللّٰهُ لَا اِلٰهَ اِلَّا هُوَ الْحَيُّ الْقَيُّوْمُ لَا تَاْخُذُهُ سِنَةٌ وَّلَا نَوْمٌ لَهُ مَا فِي السَّمٰوٰتِ وَمَا فِي الْاَرْضِ مَنْ ذَا الَّذِي يَشْفَعُ

عِنْدَهُ اِلَّا بِاِذْنِهِ يَعْلَمُ مَا بَيْنَ اَيْدِيْهِمْ وَمَا خَلْفَهُمْ وَلَا يُحِيطُوْنَ بِشَيْءٍ مِنْ عِلْمِهِ اِلَّا بِمَا شَآءَ ع وَسِعَ كُرْسِيُّهُ السَّمٰوٰتِ

وَالْاَرْضَ وَلَا يَؤُدُهُ حِفْظُهُمَا وَهُوَ الْعَلِيُّ الْعَظِيْمُ

" God ! there is no God, but He who is living and self-subsisting. Slumber and sleep do not overcome Him. Every heavenly and earthly thing belongs to Him. No one can intercede with Him save His own permission. He knows their present and past, and His knowledge does not come within their compass. His throne extends over heaven and earth, and their preservation is not burdensome to Him. He is the high, the mighty." [*Qurán*, Sûrah II.]

A Sanskrit inscription (No. XXX) of the eighth century is found, upside down, on one of the lower voussoirs of the outer arch of the south entrance of the Jâmi Masjid. The stone measures 15″ by 12½″, but it has been cut away on the left side and below the tenth line to fit it to its place. It is thus too much mutilated to allow of a connected translation, but it appears to belong to the reign of king Îśvaravarman—probably of the Maukhari dynasty of Western Magadha, and mentions a defeat of the Andhras.

CHAPTER VIII.

MINOR MASJIDS AND TOMBS.

Of the remaining masjids at Jaunpûr the following four require special notice on account of their inscriptions:—

The Masjid of **Haqîm Sulṭân Muhammad** is a small vaulted building, erected in the reign of Akbar under the governorship of **Ma'sûm Khân** by **Haqîm Sulṭân Muhammad**, in A. H. 978 (A. D. 1570), on the northern bank of the Gûmtî close to the bridge. Khair-ad-dîn states incorrectly that "it was built by **Khân Khânân Munim Khân** on the spot where prayed the faqîrs who got the credit of the dry weather and the resource of the architect" constructing the bridge.

Inscription No. XXXI is written in Persian poetry, the metre being *Mujtas*, in four lines on the north side of the Masjid of **Haqîm Sulṭân Muhammad**.

فیضی که ز لا اله الا الله است
از فضل محمد رسول الله است
این مسجد عالي که بنا کرد حکیم
اثار زمان عدل اکبر شاه است

1. The beneficence of "there is no god but God."
2. Is the gift of Muhammad, the Prophet of God.
3. This masjid which has been erected by **Haqîm**.
4. Is the sign of the justful reign of **Akbar Shâh**.

Inscription No. XXXII is written in Persian poetry, the metre being *Ramal*, in eight lines, on the south corner of the Masjid. The first line is not complete, a few characters being defaced.

× × × × × × اکبر مالك × × × ×
این بنا از لطف عام و فضل رحمن و رحیم
در زمانِ خانِ خاقان منزلت معصوم خان
آنکه هست از فیض رحمن هم رحیم و هم کریم
تا نماید ذکر نامِ باني و سالِ بنا
بر طریقی کان بود مقبول طبعِ مستقیم
دید مسکین گفت چون ابواب جنت در نظر
مسجد سلطان محمد کوست کعال و حکیم

1. (*In the reign*) of King **Akbar** (*was erected*)
2. this building by the grace of God, the merciful, the clement,

3. during the time of Ma'sûm Khân, who is equal in rank to the king of China,
4. who is, by the grace of God, merciful as well as gracious.
5. With a view to make known the name of the founder as well as the date of the building,
6. which may be agreeable to every unsophisticated mind,
7 and 8. the humble sight (*of the poet*) said: "the masjid of Sulṭân Muhammad, who is optician and doctor, looks like the gates of heaven."

The last stanza gives the date of A.H. 978 (A.D. 1570).

Inscription No. XXXIII is written in very fine Tughrâ characters round the outer frame of the *mihráb* in the central chamber of the Masjid of Haqîm Sulṭân Muhammad. Some words towards the end of the inscription are obliterated.

سلطان رحيم ولي عالم روف لا اله الا هوالرحمن الرحيم لا اله الا هوالحي القيوم لاتاخذه سنة ولا نوم

له مافي السموات وما في الارض من ذالذي يشفع عنده الا باذنه يعلم مابين ايديهم وما خلفهم ولا يحيطون

بشي من علمه الا بماشاء وسع كرسيه السموات والارض ولا يؤده حفظهما وهوا لعلي العظيم شهد الله انه

لااله الا هو وملايكة و اولوالعلم قايما بالقسط لا اله الا هوالعزيز الحكيم

× × × × ×

سبحان ربك رب العزة عما يصفون و سلام على سيد المرسلين والحمد لله رب العالمين

"The King, merciful, guardian, all-wise, clement, there is no God but He, the merciful, the clement. There is no God but He who is living and self-subsisting. Slumber and sleep do not overcome Him. Every earthly and heavenly thing belongs to Him. No one can intercede with Him save His own permission. He knows their present and past and His knowledge does not come within their compass. His throne extends over heaven and earth, and their preservation does not appear onerous to Him. He is the high, the mighty. [*Qurán*, Sûrah II.] God gives evidence that there is no God but He, who executes righteousness; and the angels and savants witness the same, there is no God but He, the mighty, the wise. [*Qurán*, Sûrah III] . . . . Thy almighty God is far above the praises attributed to Him. Peace upon the Prophet and praise to the Lord of the universe." [*Qurán*, Sûrah Sifât].

The Masjid of Nawâb Mohsin Khân in mahallâ Hammâm Darwâza, at Jaunpûr, was built in the reign of Akbar, in A. H. 975 (A. D. 1567). It is a spacious flat-roofed building, and the following inscription records its erection.

Inscription No. XXXIV is written in Persian poetry, the metre being *Ramal*, in six lines, on the south side of the masjid.

شکر کز اتوفیق حي لایموت

گشت محراب عبادت این کنشت

در جزائی این خداوند کریم
بانیش را ساخت منزل در بهشت
سال تاریخ بنایش کلکِ عقل
مسجد نواب محسن خان نوشت
سنه ۹۷۵

1. Thanks, by the grace of the self-living, who is immortal,
2. This temple has become the place of adoration (masjid);
3. In lieu of this, the bounteous God
4. Has erected a house in the Paradise for the founder;
5. The date of its foundation has been written by the pen of wisdom;
6. "Masjid Nawâb Mohsin Khân" [A. H. 975, 1567 A. D.]

The Masjid of Shâh Kabîr, in mahallâ Kartala of Jaunpûr, was built by Bâbâ Bîk in A. H. 991, or A. D. 1583, during the reign of Akbar Shâh.

Inscription No. XXXV is written in Persian poetry, the metre being *Mujtas*, in four lines, over the entrance door of the masjid.

شکر کز یاری توفیق باتمام رسید   این عبادت گه آراسته کعبه نظیر
که بود بانی این پاک مکان با با بیک   ترک قیچاق نسب قابض خورشید نظیر
بود از سال بنی نهصد و یک سال نود   که شده جامع بر روی زمین نقش پذیر
سال تاریخ تمامیش خرد کرد رقم   منزلِ پاک عبادت گه اصحاب کبیر
سنه ۹۹۱

1. Thanks, by the grace of God, this masjid like the Kâ'abâ was finished.
2. The founder of this sacred building is Bâbâ Bîk, a Turk of the Kichâk family and possessor like the sun.
3. In the year of the Prophet 991 this masjid was erected.
4. The date of its completion, written by Wisdom, is "the holy place of adoration for the 'Ashabi Kabîr." [A. H. 991, or A. D. 1583.]

The Masjid of Zahid Khân, on the south bank of the Gûmtî, east of the bridge in Miânpûr, was built in A. H. 1150, or A. D. 1737, as the following inscription shows.

Inscription No. XXXVI is written in Persian poetry, the metre being *Ramal*, in two lines, over the entrance door of the masjid.

چو زاهد خان برای طاعت حق   عجایب مسجدی عالی بپرداخت
خرد از بهر تاریخ بنایش   عبادت خانهٔ زاهد رقم کرد
سنه ۱۱۵۰

1. When Zahid Khân erected this curious masjid for the adoration of God,
2. Wisdom wrote for the date of its foundation, "Zahid's place of adoration" [A. H. 1150, or A. D. 1737].

Of the many tombs of more or less pretensions which from the time of Fîrûz Shâh to the present day have been built over former dwellers of Jaunpûr, the dargâh of Sulaimân Shâh within, and on the western side of, the Jail precincts is the most noteworthy.

It stands on a raised podium, some 65 feet square, and is built of brick coated with cement. It is square in plan and roofed by a dome; externally it measures 44′ 6″ by 44′ 6″, whilst internally the chamber tapes 29′ by 29′. Each side is pierced by three arched openings, the centre one in each case being a little larger than that on each side. The soffits of the entrance are half-domed and panelled. The face of the wall is panelled and the angles are emphasized by slender octagonal columns reaching from the plinth to the cornice. The interior of the building is somewhat dingy and unattractive. The walls are plain, but are relieved by niches and here and there by *pateræ* in glazed tile-work. The principal feature is the dome, the cupola of which is beautifully coffered and at one time was ornamented in colour, traces of which remain.

The following inscription (No. XXXVII) is written in Persian poetry, the metre being *Hazaj*, in four lines on the north end of the grave.

سلیمان شاہ بُد مقبول داور
نشُد اورا کسی در فقر همسر
ز تاریخش شمرد و لام هر بار
بگوسه مرتبه اللهُ اکبر

1. Sulaiman Shâh was the chosen of God;
2. None rivalled him in ascetism.
3. To find his date, reckon double *lám* every time,
4. Repeat thrice "God is great." [A. H. 867, A. D. 1462.]

The *abjad* powers of the letters contained in the word 'Allâh, according to *maqtúbí* or written characters, amount to 36, and according to *malfúzí*, or as the word is pronounced, amount to 66. It is distinctly said in the third *misrah* that *lám* should be reckoned twice; hence the *abjad* powers of 'Allâh-ô-Akbar according to *malfúzí* make 289, which multiplied by three gives the date A. H. 867, or A. D. 1462.

There are, besides, several other tombs of a much later date at Jaunpûr, which the people attribute to the time of Bahlol Lodî, but which are the resting places of Biluchî noblemen of the time of Akbar, *viz.*, the mausoleum of Jafir 'Alî, a platform with dome, supported on twelve slender pillars, near the Club; Husain Beg's dargâh near the Panj Sharîfa; the mausoleums of Kalîch Khân, Nawâb Ghâzî Khân, *názims* of Jaunpûr, and of Mîrza Husain Beg at Khatghara; the large mausoleum of Sher Zamân Khân, on the west bank of the Gûmtî near the bridge, being a Bagdadî octagon, or a square with the angles cut off; the dargâh of Khwâja Mîr in mahallâ Muftî and that of Faqîr Fîrûz Shâh in Sipâh mahallâ.

Enough has been said of the Jaunpûr masjids and tombs. For it will not be desired that we even catalogue the remaining masjids from that called after Mîrzâ Mîrak who repaired it, near the Sher Chabûttrâ, or the one built by Jamâl Khân, in the Sipâh mahallâ, who was *názim* of Jaunpûr in the time of Sikandar Shâh, or that built by Khân Khânân Munim Khân for Sulaimân Shekôh on the old south bank of the Gûmtî, or the long wall built by Husain Shâh for an *ídgáh*, for which, even but seventy years back the tahsîldâr of Jaunpûr had to furnish canopies and carpets. Still less will it be expected that we tell of the endowed *hammáms* which once made Jaunpûr a paradise; the buildings have long since perished, though they survived their endowments, and their sites are only known by local names. Yet once more it is necessary to express somewhat of wonder at the noble buildings on which the Musalmân invader drew so largely and whose beauty formed his style. Though we have not the frank acknowledgments of Khair-ad-dîn and his account how Ibrâhîm thought it consecration enough to knock off the head of any image and built it, face inwards, in a wall, the carved ornament discovered where any stone has fallen—whether in the wall of the dower-house, the Jâmi Masjid, the Lâl Darwâza, or the Fort—would tell plainly enough the double use of the materials. If the Atala shew less of these than other buildings, the reason probably is that there but little of the ancient building was destroyed. Yet there and everywhere, all the ornament, in gross and in detail, is purely Buddhist; the construction, the arches and domes only betray the influence of other taste. The arches are floriated with lotus buds, the spandrils relieved with full-blown lotus flowers, the bands of ornament are largely made up of lotus blossoms, in every stage, and lotus leaves from every point of view, more or less conventionalized, and even the name of God in the *qiblas* is inscribed on the Buddhist bell.

If in a visit to Jaunpûr there be melancholy, yet is that melancholy free from pain. You stand amid ruins, but ruins defiled by no painful memories. Not here does each building recall centuries of blood and lust and crime. From the pinnacles of the Jâmi Masjid you look down on the ghost of a noble city, trees growing where once stood the palaces of princes. From the mound of the Fort, now so desolate, you look down on the fair valley bright with the meanderings of the Gûmtî, adorned with trees and the thick set tombs of men, many doubtless heroic men, though their deeds be forgotten *quia carent vate sacro*. As you look down from the upper chambers into the central hall of the Jâmi Masjid, when, as the evening draws on, the deepening gloom and the dimmer distance make you feel as standing in a noble shrine of a more familiar faith, the voice of some worshipper below, echoing through the vaults, carries you back to a time when, through the same lattice, some queen looked down on king and nobles gleaming in the light of pendant lamps, with the gold and jewels of an Eastern court, as they listened to the words of some saintly philosopher seated on that very pulpit. Yet not one of these scenes recalls a crime famous in the foul annals of this world's history, and the saddest spot in the fallen city is that little cloistered court where, amid rank grass and straggling *sarífa* trees, plain blocks of stone cover the resting-places of the able Mahmûd and his noble wife, at the foot of the marble sepulchre of their son, the king, traitor, and exile, Husain.

CHAPTER IX.

ZAFARÂBÂD.

Zafarâbâd lies on the south bank of the Gûmtî four miles south-east of Jaunpûr. It is now a small agricultural village. Before the foundation of Jaunpûr it was the chief city of the neighbourhood, and up to that date it was the residence of Hindû princes of the Gaharwâr clan, as local tradition gives the last one the same name as the last king of Kanauj, Jayachchhandra. According to another tradition he was called Sakatsiṁha, and received the fort of Saktisgaṛh in the Mîrzâpûr district on his embracing Muhammadanism; an old Brâhman said that its ancient name was Mânâîchgaṛh. The walls of the old *kankar* fort of Jayachchhandra are still standing and enclose a space of 8 acres to the west of the town. Zafar Khân, the governor appointed by Fîrûz Shâh, is said to have founded a city here and to have called it Shahr Ânwar, which would give as the date of its foundation A. H. 762, or A. D. 1360; but Shaikh Bârha's masjid, on the other hand, is said to have been built or appropriated in A. H. 711, or A. D. 1311. The place has ever since been called Zafarâbâd.

A very remarkable building is the masjid known as that of Shaikh Bârha. The roof is flat and the interior is a hall 18 feet high, 9 bays deep, from east to west and 7 broad, from north to south. The outer ranges of columns are double, and plain walls close the spaces between the outmost. The square pillars are somewhat irregularly placed towards the western side; the aisle running from the door to the *qibla* is 8 feet 6 inches wide, the others 6 feet 6 inches. The substructure is of stone to above the level of the roof, and the arch which once finished the front has been of stone, but the upper half of the piers is of brick. The little remains of the spring of the arch do not seem to have any traces of the inner or recessed arch which frames the screens of the Jaunpûr masjids; but being one of the earliest and built by Hindû workmen, it conforms largely to their ideas of construction. The top of the piers is reached by a very steep stair running across the back of the arch. It never had a dome, whilst it certainly had a large arch between two piers giving a façade as lofty as that of the Atala masjid.

The stone on which Shaikh Bârha's dedication was carved fell from the front and is lost, but in a suit brought against Mr. Ommaney, a former Collector, evidence was given to show that the inscription gave the date of the building as A. H. 711, or A. D. 1311, and 'Alâ-ad-dîn Mahmûd Khiljî was said to have been the then ruler whose accession dates a century and a half later. The date refers most probably to the reign of 'Alâ-ad-dîn Muhammad Shâh.

Inscription No. XXXVIII is written in Persian characters over the *mihrâb* of the central hall of the Zafarâbâd masjid.

بسم الله الرحمن الرحيم   قل هو الله احد ه الله الصمد لم يلد و لم يولد ولم يكن له كفوا احد

لا اله الا الله محمد الرسول الله

"In the name of God, the merciful, the clement. Say, God is but one. He is the Holy God; He is not born and none born from Him, and He has no relatives. [*Qurân*, Sûrah Ikhlas.] There is no God but Allah, and Muhammad is His Prophet." [*Qurân*, Sûrah II.]

Inscription No. XXXIX is written in ten lines, mostly in Arabic and partly in Tughrâ and Shafîyah characters over the entrance door of the *mazár* or dargâh of Makhdûm Sâhib Chirâgh-i-Hind, built by Zafar Khân in the reign of Fîrûz Shâh A. H. 781, or A.D. 1379. The inscription is in Persian poetry, the metre being *Ramal;* the last two lines are partly illegible, being very much defaced.

بسم الله الرحمن الرحيم قل هوالله احد

بعهد ملك ذوالقرنين ثانى   بناء شرع را از عدل بانى

غياث دين و دنيا بوالمظفر   سليمان خاتم و جمشيد افسر

شه افاق شاهنشاه اعظم   بفيروزي جهانگير مسلم

برآمد اين حصار چرخ ايوان   كه در رفعت گذشت از فرق كيوان

برقت ختم شنبه روز بوده   ربيع الاول ماه ستوده

همايون ساعتى و وقت مسعود   ز هجري هفت صد و هشت يك بود

شد از فرمان گردون آستانه   بنا × × × × × × × مشهور زمانه

فلك يك × × × × × × ×   × × × × × × × × × × × ×

× × × × × × × × از خد اباد   × × × × × × × × × × × × ×

1. In the name of God, the merciful, the clement. Say, there is but one God.
2. In the reign of another Alexander, the founder of the law by justice,
3. Protector of religion and people, possessor of the ring of Solomon, and the crown of Jâmshêd,
4. King of the world, the great emperor, conqueror of the whole world (*Firûz Shâh*),
5. This rampart, as high as the firmament, and higher than *qaivân* (a star) was erected.
6. It was completed on Saturday, in the auspicious month of Rabi-al-awwâl,
7. At a fortunate moment and happy time in A. H. 781 [A. D. 1379].
8. By order of Him whose threshold is the sky, this world-known . . . . was erected.

9 and 10, are unintelligible.

The whole neighbourhood of Zafarâbâd abounds with *khêrâs*, the remains of Hindû palaces and temples, and with Musalmân tombs. Those to the west of the village for nearly a mile are said to be the resting-places of noblemen who with their leader, Saîd Murtaza, fell in the religious invasion of Shahâb-ad-dîn Ghorî. The place is still called "the court of the martyrs," and the tomb of Murtaza is in plan a square platform of 20 feet, with twelve Hindû pillars supporting a low entablature, above which there is a small squat dome. There are two varieties of pillars, but their shafts agree in being octagonal below, sixteen-sided in the middle, and circular at the top; they are 4 feet 9 inches in height and from 15 inches to 16 inches in diameter. The capitals are all round, the upper part being like a tulip-shaped bowl. Above these are bracket-capitals, making the total height beneath the architraves 7 feet 7 inches. Several pillars of the same pattern are used up in the dargâhs of Makhdûm Shâh and 'Asar-ad-dîn.

Near Murtaza's tomb there are a couple of small octagonal tombs, standing close together, which are commonly known as the "two sisters." These also are open buildings standing on Hindû pillars with octagonal shafts and finely-carved capitals surmounted by the usual bracket-capitals. The superstructure is also eight-sided, with openings on the alternate sides and a battlement above, from which springs a Pathân dome with rather steep sides and a flattish top.

CHAPTER X.

AYODHYA, BHUILA TAL, AND SAHET MAHET.

AYODHYÂ.

Bâbar's-Masjid at Ayodhyâ was built in A. H. 930, or A. D. 1523, by **Mîr Khân**, on the very spot where the old temple **Janmâsthânam** of **Râmachandra** was standing. The following inscriptions are of interest:

Inscription No. XL is written in Arabic characters over the central *mihrâb* of the masjid; it gives twice the Kalimah:—

لَا اِلٰهَ اِلَّا اللّٰه مُحَمَّدٌ رَسُوْلُ اللّٰه   لَا اِلٰهَ اِلَّا اللّٰه مُحَمَّدٌ رَسُوْلُ اللّٰه

"There is no God but 'Allâh, Muhammad is His Prophet." [*Qurân*, Sûrah II.]

Inscription No. XLI is written in Persian poetry, the metre being **Ramal**, in six lines on the *mimbâr*, right-hand side of the masjid.

بمنشلی با بر خدیو جهان
بشانیکه با کاخ گردون عنان
بنا کرده این خانهٔ پائدار
امیر سعادت نشان میر خان
بماند همیشه چنا بانیش
چنان شهریار زمین و زمان

1. By order of **Bâbar**, the king of the world,
2. This firmament-like, lofty,
3. Strong building was erected
4. By the auspicious noble **Mîr Khân**.
5. May ever remain such a foundation,
6. And such a king of the world.

The letters of this inscription have been mixed together by the copyist, and are therefore very indistinct.

Inscription No. XLII is written in Persian poetry, the metre being **Ramal**, in ten lines, above the entrance door of the masjid. A few characters of the second and the whole third lines are completely defaced.

بسم الله الرحمن الرحيم

بنام آنکه × × × × × × ×   کند خالق بتلم جاوداني
× × × × × ×   × × × × × ×
چنان شاهنشه مشهور اقلیم   زمین را چون مثال شادماني
دران حضرت یکی میری معظم   که خاقان دولت و فعفور ثانی
بنای عهد دین تاریخ میمون   که نهصد سی بود هجرت بداني

خدايا در جهان باشاه بادا   بچتر و تخت بخت زندگاني
فشاند در جهان با بر گل خير   كند در دور گيتي كامراني
مشير سلطنت تدبير ملكش   كزين مسجد حصارى هست باني
هذالقطعه التاريخ و صفت مسجد بخط نحيف عبد ضعيف فتح‌الله غوري محرر

1 In the name of God, the merciful, the clement.

2 In the name of him who... ..; may God perpetually keep him in the world.

3 . . . .

4 Such a sovereign who is famous in the world, and in person of delight for the world.

5 In his presence one of the grandees who is another king of Turkey and China,

6 Laid this religious foundation in the auspicious Hijra 930.[1]

7 O God! may always remain the crown, throne and life with the king.

8 May Bâbar always pour the flowers of happiness; may remain successful

9 His counsellor and minister who is the founder of this fort masjid.

10 This poetry, giving the date and eulogy, was written by the lazy writer and poor servant Faṭh-allâh-Ghorî, composer.

The old temple of Râmachandra at Janmâsthânam must have been a very fine one, for many of its columns have been used by the Musalmâns in the construction of Bâbar's masjid. These are of strong, close-grained, dark-coloured or black stone, called by the natives *kasauti*, "touch-stone slate," and carved with different devices. They are from seven to eight feet long, square at the base, centre and capital, and round or octagonal intermediately.

Inscription No. XLIII is written in Tughrâ characters on a fragment of red sandstone, brought from the ruined Masjid of Aurangzîb, built on the site of an old temple, called Svargadvâramandiram. The original stone is at present in the Faizâbâd Local Museum.

لاَ الٰهَ الا اللّٰهُ مُحَمَّدٌ رَسُوْلُ اللّٰه بارِكْ وَ سلّمْ و صلى

"There is no God but Allâh, and Muhammad is His Prophet. May peace, benediction and blessings be upon him!" [*Qurán.*]

Inscription No. XLIV is written in twenty incomplete lines on a white sandstone, broken off at either end, and split in two parts in the middle. It is dated Saṁvat 1241, or A. D. 1184, in the time of Jayachchhandra of Kanauj, whose praises it records for erecting a Vaishṇava temple, from whence this stone was originally brought and appropriated by Aurangzîb in building his masjid known as Tretâ-kî-Thâkur. The original slab was discovered in the ruins of this Masjid, and is now in the Faizâbâd Local Museum.

Bhuîla Tâl.

This place lies 18 miles north-west from Bastî and 25 miles north-east from Ayodhyâ and has been identified by Mr. Carlleyle[2] with Kapilavastu, the birthplace of Śâkyamuni, which identification General Cunningham approves of. After

[1] The *Oudh Gazetteer*, Vol. I, page 6, gives the date of the completion of this Masjid as A. H. 935, or A. D. 1528; the word *hijra* in the inscription having probably been read *panj*. But this is incorrect, as the metre shows.

[2] Cunningham, *Archæological Reports*, Vol. XII, page 112 seqq.

a careful inspection of all the places identified by Mr. Carlleyle, I come to the conclusion that this spot cannot be the Kie-pi-lo-fa-su-tu (Kapilavastu) of Hiuen Tsiang, on the following grounds:—

1. Hiuen Tsiang states "that the country of Buddha's birth is about 4,000 li in circuit," whilst the tract of land lying between the Ghâgrâ river and the Gaṇḍakâ, from Ayodhyâ to the confluence of these rivers, gives a circuit of 550 miles, which would represent upwards of 600 miles by road.
2. The places excavated and identified by Mr. Carlleyle as the principal palace of Śuddhodana Râjâ, the bed-chamber of the queen Mahâmâyâ, and the stûpa of Asita the Ṛishi, are so insignificant that they cannot be the remains of the ruins mentioned by Hiuen Tsiang.
3. The circular tank about 340 feet to the south of Bhuîla Tâl and still called, according to Mr. Carlleyle, 'Hâthîkuṇḍ' or 'Hâthîgadh,' was identified by him with the *hastigarta*, or 'fallen elephant ditch' of Hiuen Tsiang, and General Cunningham is perfectly convinced that this is the spot indicated in the Chinese text. The chaukidâr of the neighbouring village Nyagrodha, however, states that the name Hâthîkuṇḍ or Hâthîgadh was first given to this tank by Mr. Carlleyle himself, and that this name was utterly unknown in that part of the country before the arrival of Mr. Carlleyle.
4. Mr. Carlleyle indicates Krakuchchhanda Buddha's fabled birth-place at Nagara, 7½ miles to the north-west of Kapilavaṣtu, whilst it must be sought 8 miles to the south-east of that place, as Fa-Hian, visiting this place after leaving Śrâvastî, went north about 8 miles, then east 8 miles to Kapilavastu.

From this it is evident that Bhuîla Tâl is *not* the ancient site of Kapilavastu. Our knowledge about the position of Kapilavastu may at present be reduced to this: that it lay on the route from the Buddhist cities of eastern Gorakhpûr to the Buddhist Śrâvastî (Saheṭ-Maheṭ) of the Gondâ district, and that route probably passed between the Ghâgrâ and Raptî rivers.

Saheṭ-Maheṭ.

A vast collection of ruins on the south bank of the Raptî, 12 miles north-west from Balrâmpûr and 42 north-west from Gondâ, was identified by General Cunningham[1] as the remains of the ancient Buddhist city Śrâvastî, whose site had already been conjecturally fixed by Lassen within a few miles of that place, but to the north of the river.

Notwithstanding the excavations made by General Cunningham in 1862-63 and by Dr. W. Hoey, C.S., in 1884-85, as yet very little is known of these most interesting ruins, which must contain relics which would do much to elucidate some of the darkest and most interesting periods of Indian history. I have no doubt that a thorough and properly conducted excavation would be of great success and yield many Buddhist and Jaina relics, and especially as the Mahârâṇî of Balrâmpûr is willing to grant a large subvention for this purpose; but it ought to be gone about in a scientific method.

[1] *Archæological Reports*, Vol. I, 330 seqq.; Vol. XI, 78 seqq.

During my stay I collected at Saheṭ eight baked and two unbaked clay seals containing in five lines, and in one instance in fifteen lines, the Buddhist creed formula in Devanâgarî characters of the seventh and eighth century; one lac seal, inscribed with *juvasa* in Gupta characters; one unbaked clay seal of a Buddhist monastery, as it would seem to be from its appearance and place where found at Saheṭ, inscribed *atrâsa* in Gupta characters; one lac seal found outside the west gate of Maheṭ, inscribed *govanandasa* in Gupta characters; two lac seals inscribed *navatipukayasa* in Gupta characters with the *svastika* and Aśoka leaves above; one lac seal, inscribed *ashṭavṛiddha* in Gupta characters; one baked clay seal representing a chaitya; and two copper coins of Phaguni and Bhûmi Mitra—of the so-called Śuṅga dynasty. That Buddhism was still flourishing at Śrâvastî in the seventh and eighth century is proved by the many baked and unbaked clay seals found there, inscribed in characters of that time.

Jainism was very strong in Śrâvastî in the eleventh century, as is shown by the following Jain statues excavated by Dr. W. Hoey and now placed in the Lucknow Provincial Museum: a well-carved statue of Vimalanâthadêva (sitting), dated Saṁvat 1133, Jyaishṭa su.di. 3; another (standing), Saṁvat 1182; a statue of Neminâtha (sitting), dated Saṁvat 1125; a statue of Aṁśanâtha (standing), Saṁvat 1112; and a statue of Ṛishabhanâtha (standing), Saṁvat 1124.

The most interesting fact, however, is the discovery of an inscription (No. XLV) at Maheṭ, which shows that Buddhism was still flourishing at the ancient site of Śrâvastî in the beginning of the thirteenth century, and that it was not extinguished in Magadha at that time.

This inscription was found by Dr. W. Hoey during his excavations in 1884-85 at Maheṭ, buried under the ruins of a Buddhist building erected on the old site of Buddha's *vihâra* in Jetavana. The inscribed sandstone measures 2′ 9″ by 1′ 3″, and records in eighteen lines, in Saṁvat 1276 (A. D. 1219), the erection of a convent for Buddhist ascetics at the town of Ajâvṛisha by Vidhyâdhara, the fifth of six sons of Janaka and Jijjâ, and grandson of Bilvaśiva, of the Śrî Pûrva-Vâstavya family. Janaka, the father of Vidhyâdhara, is described as the counsellor of Gôpâla, the ruler of Gâdhipura, or Kanauj; and Vidhyâdhara appears to have held a similar position under the Prince Madana, probably a successor of Gôpâla. The town of Ajâvṛisha is said to have been built by Mândhâta of the solar race and to have its protection entrusted to Karkoṭa (*Śiva*); this proves that the old Buddhist name of the place, *viz.*, Śrâvastî, must have been lost very early. It is also interesting in another respect,—because it speaks of the Hindû kingdom of Kanauj as if it were still in existence, though we know that Jayachchhandra of Kanauj was defeated and his capital taken by the Musalmâns in A. D. 1193. The original slab is now in the Lucknow Provincial Museum.

The preservation of the slab is perfect. The mistakes made by the engraver are few and unimportant and admit of easy correction. In respect to orthography we have to notice:—(1) the frequent use of the dental sibilant for the palatal in ten cases; (2) the constant occurrence of *ba* being denoted by the sign for *va;* (3) the persistent doubling of *k, g, j, t, m, l* in conjunction with a preceding *r*.

The characters are Devanâgarî of the twelfth century; the *anusvâra*, instead of being written above the *akshara* after which it is pronounced, is eleven times written after it, with the sign of *virâma* below the *anusvâra*. The language is Sanskṛit, and the inscription is in verse throughout, excepting the introductory blessing and the date at the end. From a grammatical point of view there is the wrong form *avamanya*, the wrong compound *tatpañchamaḥ*, and the unusual derivatives *janîna* and *udarambharîṇa*.

TEXT.[1]

[L. 1.] ओं नमो वीतरागाय ॥ [2]भारानष्टनियम्य दिक्षधिपतीनायोन्य सत्वोदये दुर्ल्लंघ्यास्त्ववमन्य संवररिपोराज्ञाम्बराख्यहृत: । उद्दर्त्तुं यतते स्म य: करुणया त्रीसा -

[2.] क्यासिंहो [3]अगद्दोधिं प्राप्य च] बुद्धतामभिगत: सत्वां परित्रायतां ॥ [१॥] [4]संसारांभोधिताराय तारासुत्तारलोचनां । वन्दे गीर्व्वाणवाणीनां भारतीमधिदेवताम् ॥ [२॥]

[3.] [5]मांधाताख्य: प्रभुजिष्णुक्रतुल्यो वंसे भानोर्भानुतेजोतिसायी । नित्यानन्दी साधु भोक्ता त्रिलोकीं राज्ञामाद्यश्चक्रवर्त्ती वभूव ॥ [३॥] [6]स्वेच्छां भ्राम्यन्कदाचित्सर -

[4.] सिरुहरजोराजिचित्रीकृताम्भ: सम्यग्दृष्ट्वा सरोन्तर्मंदकलसकु[7]निप्रातरावाभिरम्यं । कर्त्तुं कीर्त्तेर्वितानं सुचरितमुदितो न्यद्विरापूर्य यत्नात्कर्कोटाधीनरा -

[5.] थं स्वपुरमिदमथो निर्ममेजाहृपाख्यं ॥ [४॥] [8]तस्मिन्नभूवन्धनिनोतिधन्या: श्रीपूर्व्ववास्तव्यकुलप्रदीपा: । अद्यापि यद्वंसभवैर्यशोभिर्व्वंगन्ति शुभ्रैर्धवली -

[6]. क्रियन्ते ॥ [५॥] [9]तेषामभूदभिजने जलधाविवेन्दुरिंदुद्युति: प्रथितविल्वशिवाभिधान: । यस्य स्मरारिचरणांबुजवत्सलस्य लक्ष्मीर्हिजातिसुजनार्थिजनोपभो -

[7.] ग्या ॥ [६॥] [10]सौजन्यांबुनिधेरुदारचरितप्रत्यक्षमानेनस: साधूनामुदयैकधाम जननीस्थानं श्रिय: सत्वभू: । तस्यासीज्जनको जनीनहृदय: पुत्र: सताम -

[8.] ग्रणीर्मान्यो गाधिपुराधिपस्य सचिवो गोपालनामा: सुधी: ॥ [७॥] [11]तेनोच्चकैरभिजनाम्बुनिधे: प्रसूता लक्ष्मीरिवाच्युतविभूषणकान्तमूर्त्ति: । आनन्दकन्दज -

[9.] ननी जननीकुलानां जिज्जेति संभृतकुलस्थितिरोपयेमे ॥ [८॥] [12]ताभ्यामभूवंस्तनया: षडेव षड्भिर्मुखैरेकतनुर्यं एक: । ज्यायान्सुत: पिप्पटनामधे -

[10.] यो धीमानिवाम्बिप्रभव: शिवाभ्यां ॥ [८॥] [13]तत्पंचम: पंचसराणुकारी तयोस्तनूजोतनुकीर्त्तिकान्द: । विद्याववोधादनुकीर्त्यते यो विद्याधरो नाम यथार्थ -

[11.] नामा ॥ [१०॥] [14]रसाधिकमभिव्यापि गिरीशचरणाश्रितं । हंसीव मानसं यस्य जहाति न भारती ॥ [११॥] [15]माधुर्यं मधुनी सुधा हिमरुचेरानन्दमेधाविता मि -

[12.] [16]ध्येवाम्बुनिधेर्गभीरिमगुणस्तुंगत्वमद्रेरलं । यस्यैकैकगुणाधिरोहणगिरि: सौजन्यसांद्रोल्लसत्पीयषैकनिधेर्म्मुणिन गुणिन: सर्व्वेप्यधश्चक्रिरे ॥ [१२॥] [17]यस्मै

[1] From the original stone.

[2] L. 1. Metre Śârdûlavikrîḍita. Read: सत्वोदये दुर्लंघ्यान्यवमत्य श्रम्बर°; त्रीसा -.

[3] L. 2. Read: जगद्वोधिं; बुद्धतामभिगत: ;

[4] Metre Śloka (Anushṭubh).

[5] L. 3. Metre Śâlinî. Read: वंशे, °तेजोतिशायी; बभूव;

[6] Metre Sragdharâ.

[7] L. 4. Read: °शकुनि°;

[8] L. 5. Metre Upajâti. Read: यद्वंश°, शुभ्रैर्धवली -

[9] L. 6. Metre Vasantatilakâ. Read: °बिल्व°, °चरणाम्बु°.

[10] L. 7. Metre Śârdûlavikrîḍita. Read: सौजन्याम्बु°, सत्वभू:

[11] L. 8. Metre Vasantatilakâ. Read: अभिजनाम्बु°.

[12] L. 9. Metre Indravajrâ.

[13] L. 10. Metre Upajâti. Read: पञ्चशराणुकारी; विद्यावबोधादनुकीर्त्यते.

[14] L. 11. Metre Śloka (Anushṭubh).

[15] Metre Śârdûlavikrîḍita.

[16] L. 12. Read: ध्येवाम्बु°; °सान्द्रोल्लसत्°.

[17] Metre Vasantatilakâ.

[13.] गजागमरहस्यविदे गजानामानन्दनीं कलयति धुरसुराय । भूपालमौलितिलको मदन: प्रदानमानादिभि: क्षितिपति: स्तवयां [18]बभूव ॥ [१३॥] [19]देवा -

[14.] लयै: प्रथयता निजकीर्त्तिसुधै: [20]पुष्पद्विजव्रजसुदेतुमलम्बभूव । येनार्ज्जितं द्रविणमार्त्तजनोपकारि जीवातुसम्भृतसुदासुदरभरीणं ॥ [१४॥] [21]सत्वसार्थप -

[15.] रित्राणकृतकायपरिग्रह: । अभूदभूतपूर्व्वोयं [22]बोधिसत्व इवापर: ॥ [१५॥] [23]बालभ्रातलतोदयन विगलद्रागादिदोषाश्रयमोक्षच्छमनसा विचार्य्य बहुसो

[16.] मध्यस्थतां सौगते[।] तेनाराधितसत्पथेन यमिनामानन्दमूलालयो [24]निर्म्मप्योत्ससृजे विहारविधिना कीर्त्तेरिवैकाश्रय: ॥ [१६॥] [25]सद्दोधवंशचरि -

[17.] तस्य नयैकधाम्नश्चंद्रावदातहृदय: सुमति: कलावान् । अस्य प्रियेषु निरत: [26]सुभगंभविष्णु: सम्बन्धवन्धुहृदयी विदधे प्रसस्तिम् ॥ [१७॥]

[18.] संवत् १२७६ [॥]

TRANSLATION.

Oṁ!

Adoration to him who is free from passions!

(Verse 1.) May the illustrious Śâkya lion protect you!—he who, having at the rising of truth restrained the eight Mâras, (*and*) attracted to himself the lords over the (*eight*) regions, having treated with contempt the difficult-to-be-transgressed words of command of the enemy Śambara, full of zeal through compassion exerted himself to deliver the world; and who, having reached the Bodhi tree, attained the Buddhahood!

(2.) To cross the ocean of worldly existence, I adore the saving Bhâratî, whose eyes have protruding pupils,[27] the goddess presiding over the utterances of the gods.

(3.) In the race of the Sun there was, surpassing the splendour of the Sun, the universal sovereign, the first of kings, named Mândhâtṛi, conquering the enemies, equal to Indra, ever gladdening, well protecting the three worlds.

(4.) Once upon a time, roaming about at his pleasure, he saw a pleasant lake whose waters were variegated with lines of the pollen of lotuses, (*and*) charming with the cries of flocks of sweetly-singing birds in it; and having strenuously filled it with earth, he, who delighted in good conduct, to make a canopy of fame, then built this town of his, named Ajâvṛisha, the protection of which was entrusted to Karkoṭa (*Śiva*).

(5.) In it there were (*born*) wealthy (*and*) very fortunate (*men*), lights of the illustrious Pûrva-Vâstavya family, by the splendid fame of whose race the worlds are rendered white even now.

(6.) As the moon (*is born*) from the ocean, so in their family there was (*born a personage,*) shining like the moon, whose name Bilvaśiva was famous; devoted as he was to the lotus-feet of the enemy of Kâma, (*i.e., Śiva*), his wealth was an object of enjoyment to the twice-born, to virtuous people, and to supplicants.

[18] L. 13. Read: बभूव.

[19] Metre Vasantatilakâ.

[20] L. 14. Read: पुष्पद्विजव्रजसुदेतुमलं बभूव.

[21] Metre Śloka (Anushṭubh). Read: सत्त्व०.

[22] L. 15. Read: बोधिसत्त्व.

[23] Metre Sârdûlavikriḍita. Read: बाल्यप्राणलतोदयेन; बहुशो.

[24] L. 16. Read: निर्माप्योत्ससृजे.

[25] Metre Vasantatilakâ. Read सद्दोध०.

[26] L. 17 Read: सुभगम्भविष्णु:; सम्बन्धबन्धुहृदयी; प्रशस्तिं.

[27] The original alludes to the Târâs, or Śaktis of the Dhyâni-Buddhas, one of whom is called *Lochanâ*.

(7.) He an ocean of benevolence, who was counteracting sins by his noble conduct, had a son, Janaka, a unique home of the good, a birthplace of fortune, a site of goodness, with a heart kind to people, the foremost of the good, the honoured wise counsellor of the ruler of Gâdhipura (Kanauj), named Gopâla.

(8.) He, who well maintained the prosperity of his family, married the daughter of a noble race, named Jijjâ, who was causing joy to her mother's family, (*and who*), inasmuch as her lovely body possessed imperishable ornaments, was like Lakshmî, born from the ocean, whose lovely body beautifies Achyuta (Vishṇu).

(9.) From these two there were born no less than six sons, just as the intelligent progeny of fire, called Pippata[28] who one, with one body, is endowed with six faces, (*was born*), as the elder son, from Śiva and his consort.

(10.) Their fifth son of those (*six*), resembling the five-arrowed (*Kâma*) (*and*) the root of no slight fame, who is celebrated for his knowledge of wisdom, is named, with an appropriate name, Vidyâdhara "the holder of wisdom."

(11.) Whose comprehensive mind, full of taste (*and*) attached to the feet of Śiva, Bhâratî never abandoned, just as the swan never leaves the extensive Mânasa lake, full of water (*and*) situated at the foot of the lord of mountains (*Himâlaya*).

(12.) Vain is the sweetness of honey (*and*) the proficiency in (*creating*) joy of the cool-rayed (*moon*); a sham indeed is the quality of depth of the ocean (*and*) the height of the mountain; (*but*) enough! by the excellent qualities of this mountain for the ascent of every single excellency, of this unique receptacle of the abundant sparkling nectar of benevolence, everything whatever that is endowed with excellent qualities has been surpassed!

(13.) Him, who knew the secret doctrine regarding elephants, (*and*) who, unrestrained, bore the burden of elephants that was causing pleasure (*to him*), the head-ornament of princes, the lord of the earth, Madana, sought to attach to himself by gifts, honours, and so forth.

(14.) The wealth acquired by him, who spread his fame aloft by (*building*) temples,—(*wealth*) which gave relief to people in distress, (*and*) filled the bellies of those filled with joy at (*the receipt of*) food,—was sufficient to exceed the multitude of the twice-born supported (*by it*).

(15.) He was as it were another Bodhisattva, such as had never existed before, having assumed a human body for the protection of the multitude of living beings.

(16.) Elevated by the knowledge of the soul, (*and*) with a mind rising above the attachment to passion, and of other sins of which he was getting rid, having again and again pondered on the indifference towards the doctrine of Sugata, he, having resorted to the good path, caused to be built and granted to the ascetics, after the manner of convents, a dwelling causing joy, a unique home of it as if it were of (*his own*) fame.

(17.) Taking delight in whatever is dear to him, the unique home of prudence, whose conduct is an object of adoration for people of true knowledge, Udayin, (*his*) kinsman by association, whose heart is pure like the moon, (*and who is*) wise (*and*) accomplished (*and*) becoming prosperous, has composed (*this*) eulogy.

(L. 18.) The Saṁvat (*year*) 1276, or A. D. 1219.

[28] According to this version, Pippaṭa is apparently another name of Skanda or Kârttikeya; there is, however, clearly an allusion to the legend according to which Kârttikeya was the son of Śiva without the intervention of Pârvatî, Śiva's generative energy being cast into the fire.

INDEX.

PLATE IV.

JAUNPUR: ATALA MASJID,—GROUND PLAN.

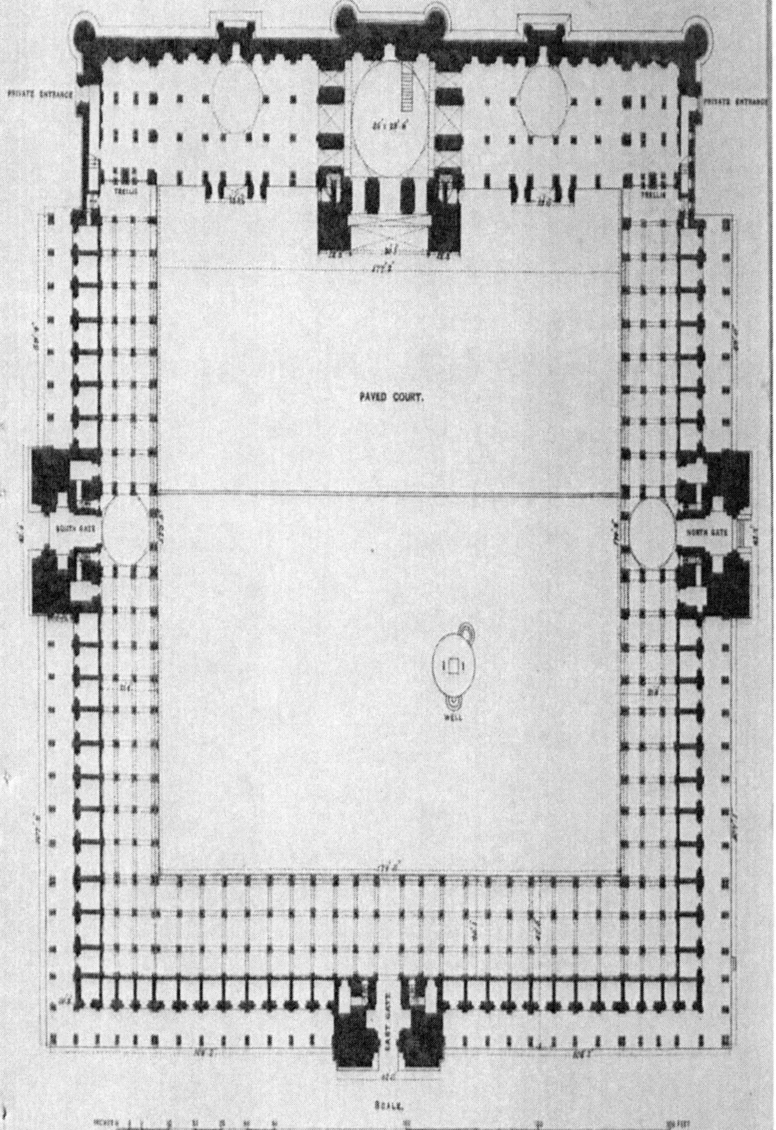

Archaeological Survey of India

EDMD. W. SMITH.
Architectural Asst.

PLATE V.

JAUNPUR: ATALA MASJID,—UPPER PLAN.

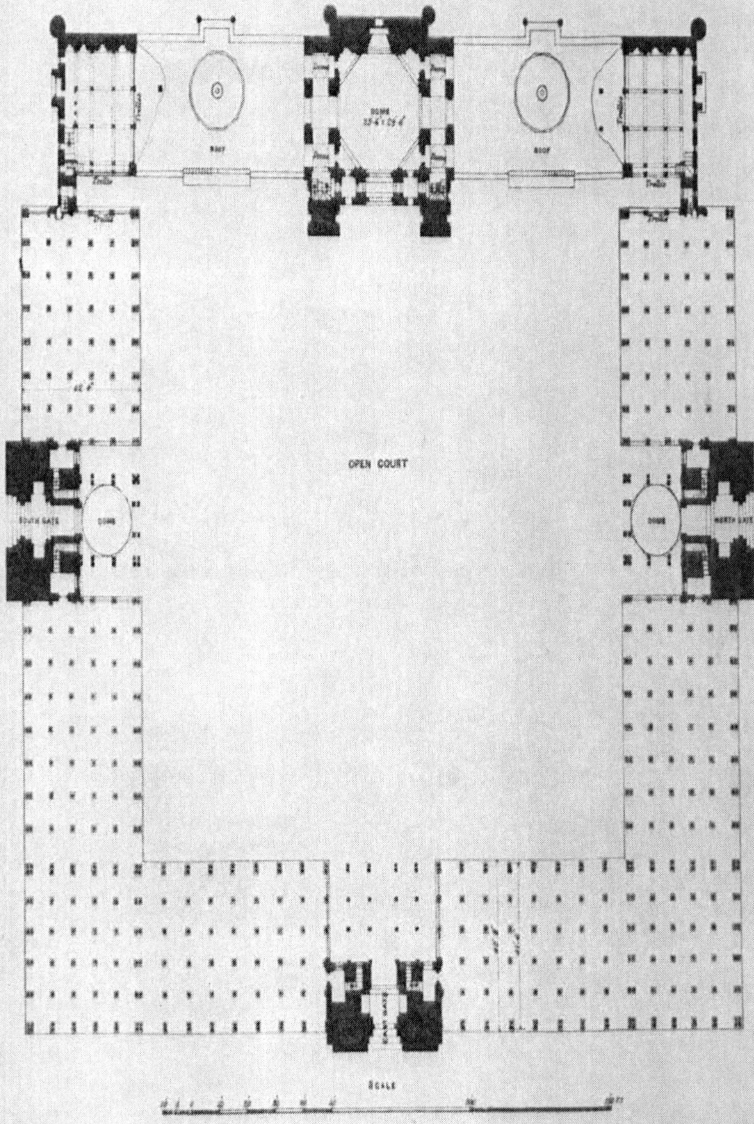

EDMD. W. SMITH,
Architectural Asst.

Archæological Survey of India

Lithographed at the Survey of India Offices, Calcutta, March [illegible]

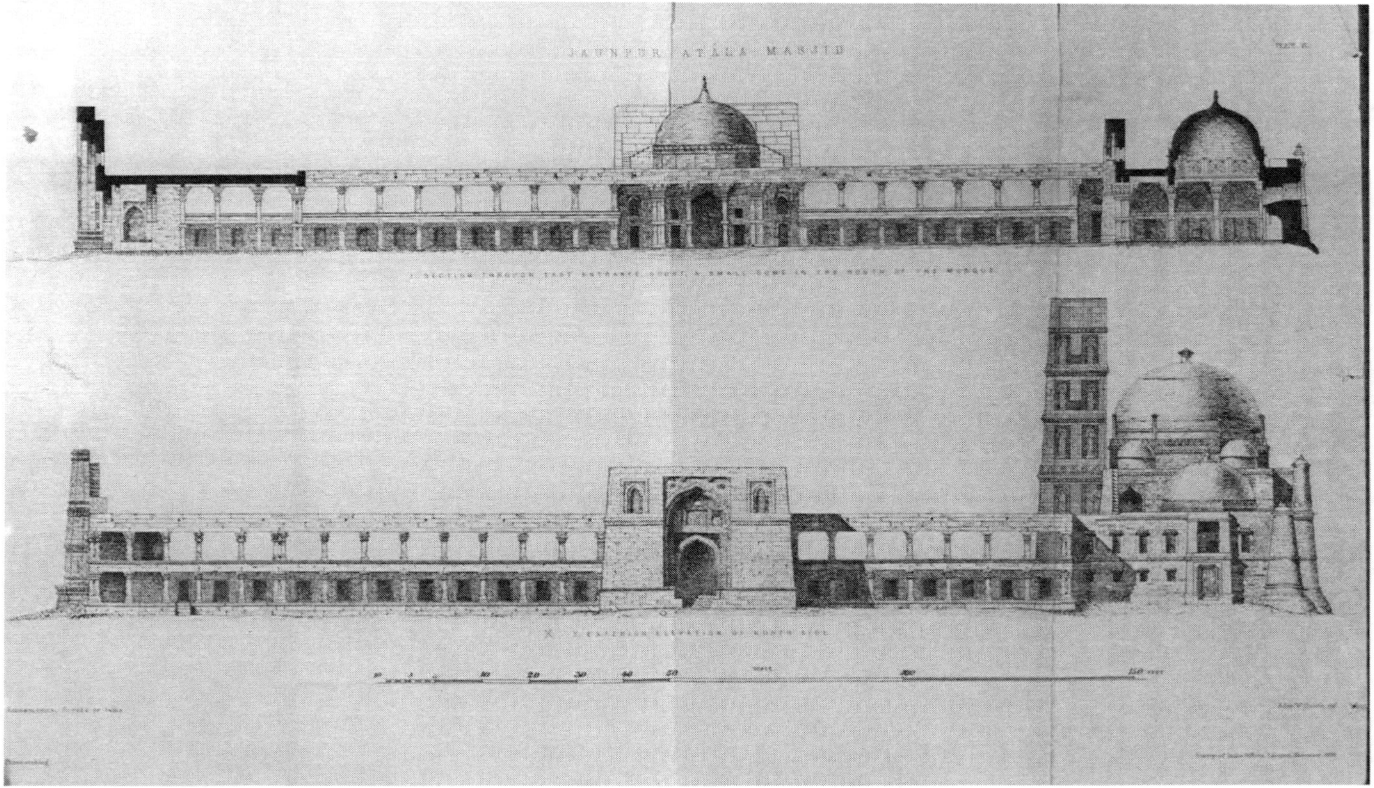
JAUNPUR ATALA MASJID

PLATE VII.

JAUNPUR: ATALA MASJID.

HALF ELEVATION OF PRINCIPAL PROPYLON AND HALF SECTION OF GREAT DOME.

SCALE

Archæological Survey of India

Photo-Lithographed at the Survey of India Offices, Calcutta, March

PLATE VIII.

JAUNPUR: ATALA MASJID.

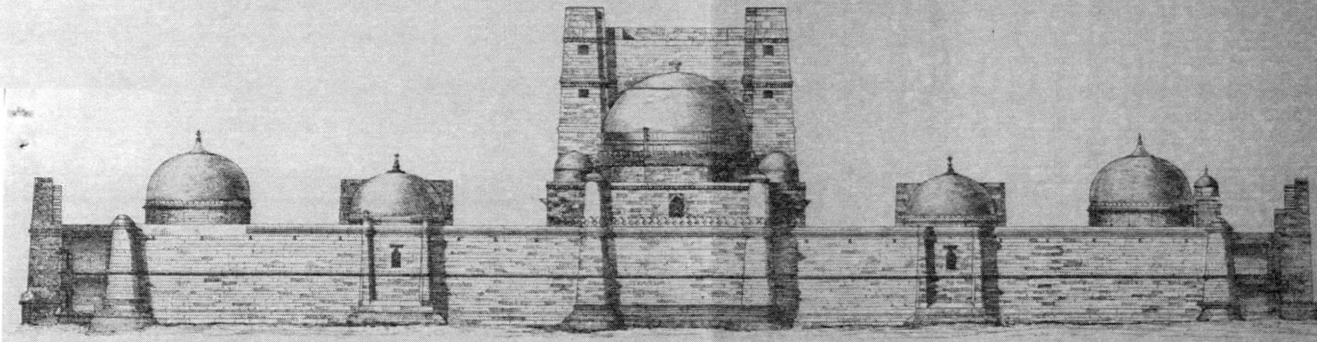

WEST OR BACK ELEVATION.

JAUNPUR: ATALA MASJID.—TWO BAYS UNDER THE GREAT DOME.

Archaeological Survey of India.

Photo-Lithographed at the Survey of India Offices, Calcutta, May 18[illegible].

E. W. Smith,
Architectural Asst.

PLATE X

JAUNPUR: ATALA MASJID,—SIDE ELEVATION OF CENTRAL ARCHED ENTRANCE.

Archæological Survey of India

Photo-Lithographed at the Survey of India Offices, Calcutta, March

E. W. SMITH,
Architectural Asst.

JAUNPUR: ATALA MASJID.

PLATE XI.

Survey of India Offices, Calcutta, December [illegible]

Archaeological Survey of India

SCALE.

INCHES 12 ... 1 ... 2 ... 3 ... 4 FEET.

EDMD. W. SMITH, del.

CARVED ROOF OF CENTRAL ENTRANCE TO THE GREAT DOME.

PLATE XII.

JAUNPUR: ATALA MASJID,—PRINCIPAL MIHRAB AND MIMBAR.

Archaeological Survey of India.

Photo-Lithographed at the Survey of India Offices, Calcutta, July 18..

JAUNPUR: ATALA MASJID.

PLATE XIII.

SCALE.

INCHES. FOOT.

Archaeological Survey of India.

TYMPANUM OF THE RECESSES ON EACH SIDE THE PRINCIPAL MIHRAB.

EDMD. W. SMITH.

PLATE XIV.

JAUNPUR: ATALA MASJID

HALF ELEVATION OF NORTH ENTRANCE.

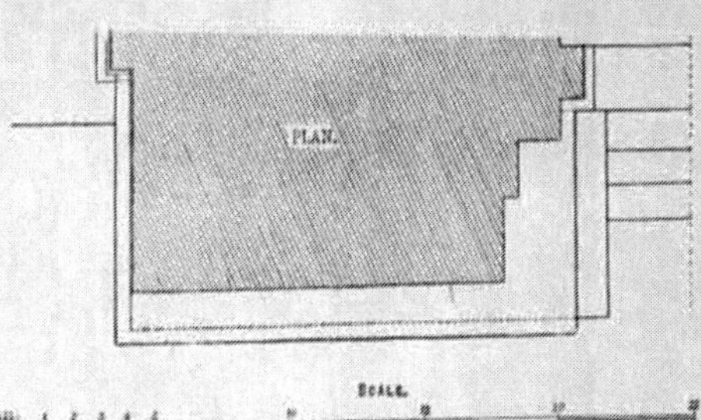

PHOTOZINCOGRAPHED AT THE SURVEY OF INDIA OFFICES, CALCUTTA, APRIL [illegible]

Archæological Survey of India.

EDMD. W. SMITH,
Archæological Asst.

JAUNPUR: ATALA MASJID

Half Elevation of Principal or East Entrance

PLATE XV.

Archaeological Survey of India

Photolithographed at the Survey of India Offices, Calcutta, March 18[illegible]

E. W. SMITH,
Architectural Asst.

JAUNPUR: ATALA MASJID.

South Propylon of the Masjid.

SCALE

INCHES 12 6 0 1 2 3 4 5 10 15 20 FEET

Archaeological Survey of India.

E. W. SMITH,
Architectural Asst.

Photo-Lithographed at the Survey of India Offices, Calcutta, May 18[illegible].

JAUNPUR ATALA MASJID

Scale of Feet

PANEL ON THE SOUTHERN SMALLER PROPYLON OF THE MOSQUE

PLATE XVIII

JAUNPUR: ATALA MASJID,—MIHRAB UNDER SMALL DOME IN THE SOUTH OF THE MOSQUE

JAUNPUR: ATALA MASJID

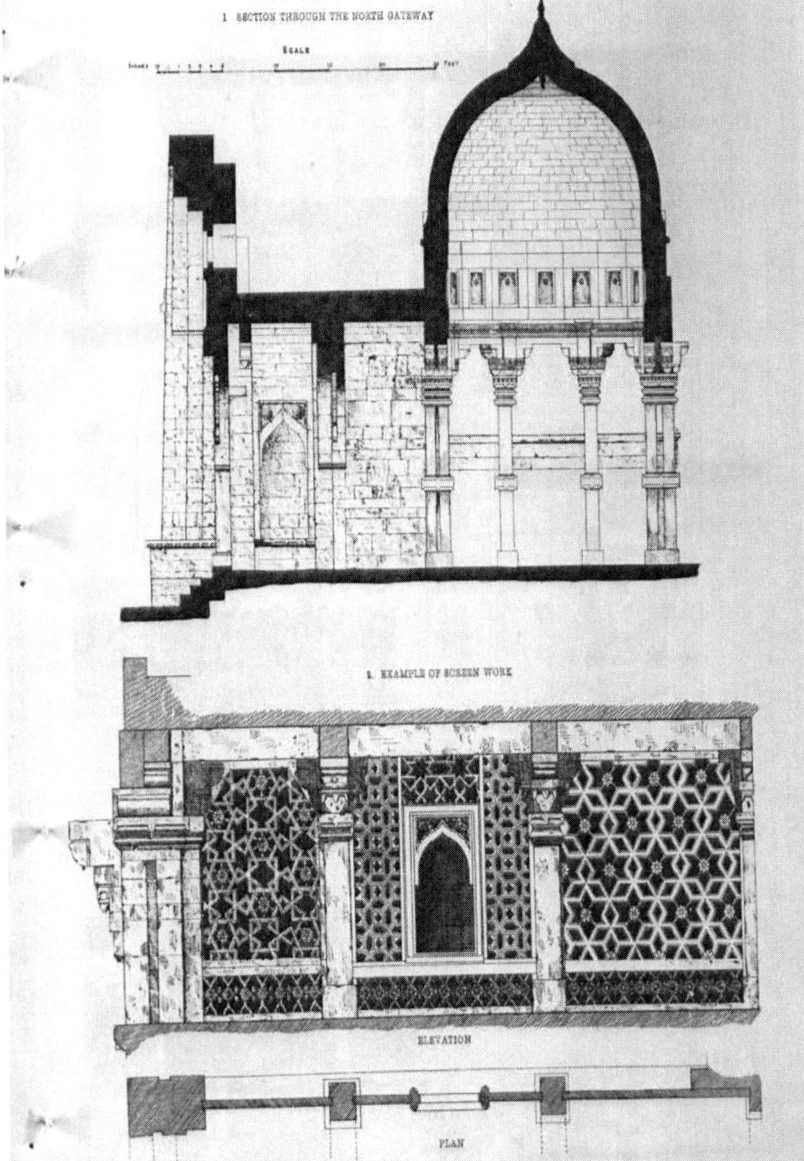

PLATE XX

JAUNPUR: ATALA MASJID

1 SECTION THROUGH THE CORRIDORS

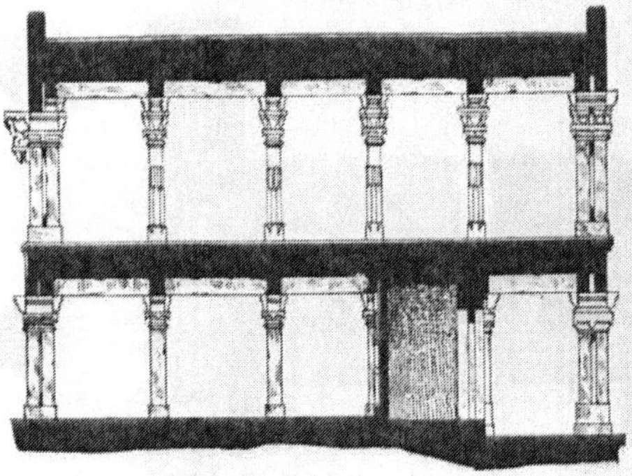

4

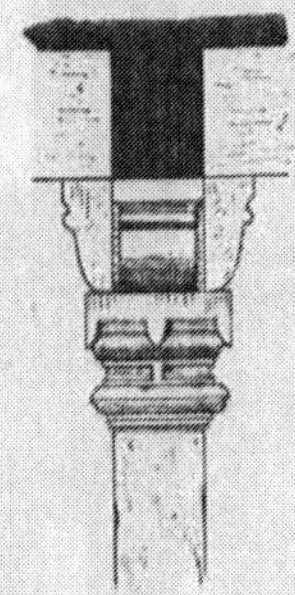

2 ELEVATION

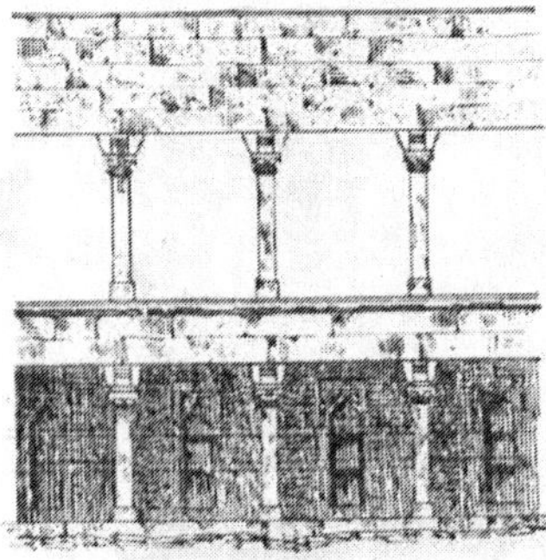

5 PILLAR

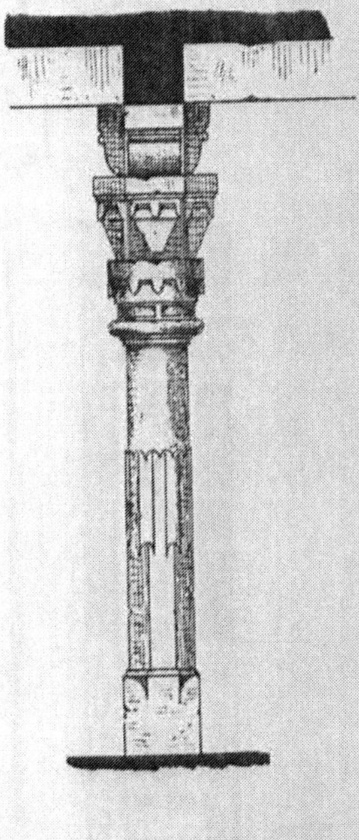

3

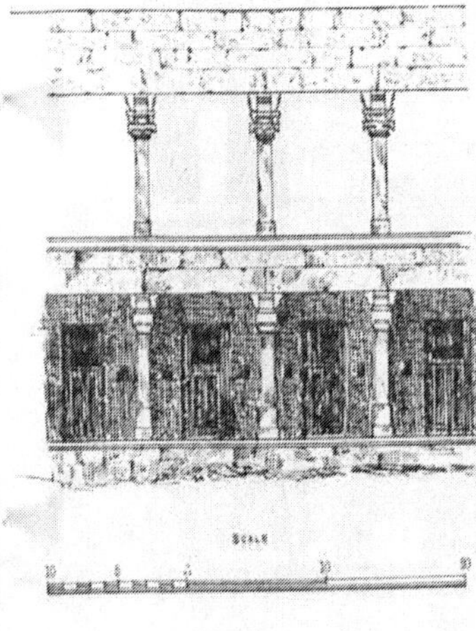

SCALE

10 5 0 10 20 FEET

SCALE

12 6 0 1 2 3 4 FEET

E. W. SMITH
Architectural Asst.

Photo-Lithographed at the Survey of India Offices, Calcutta, March [illegible]

Archaeological Survey of India.

JAUNPUR: ATALA MASJID

PLATE XXI

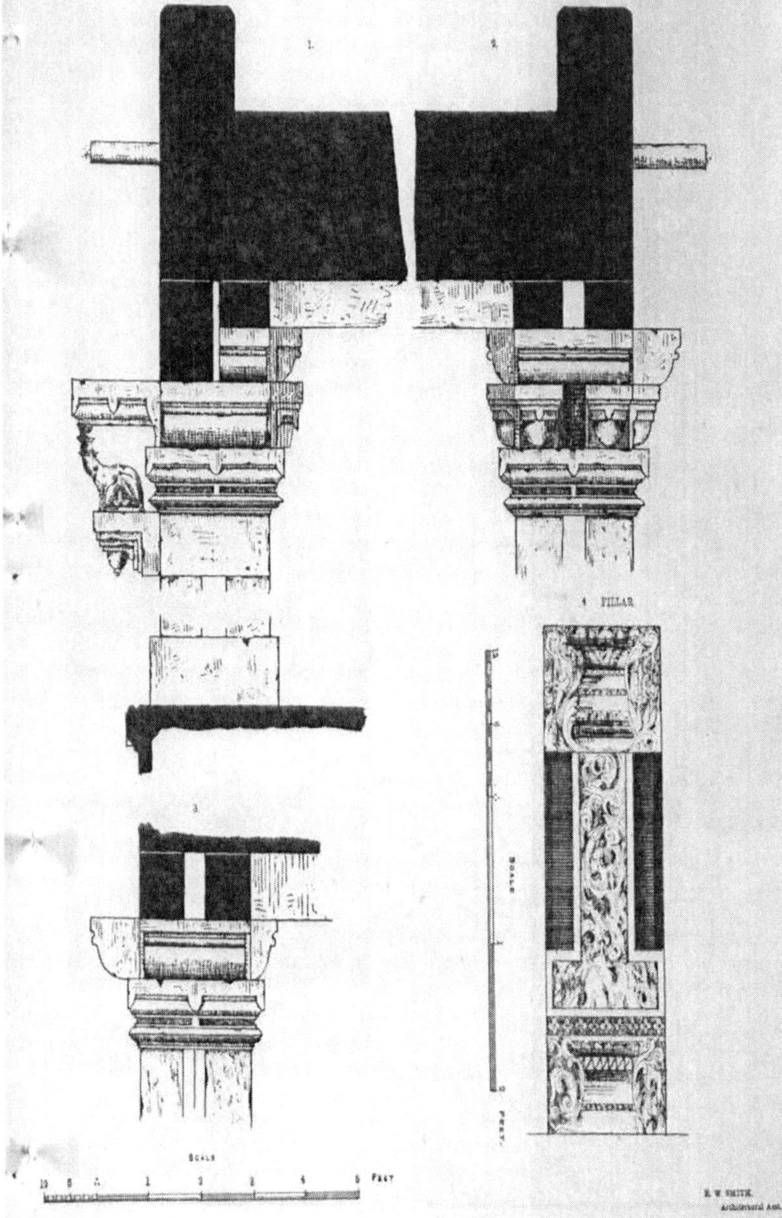

E. W. SMITH.
Architectural Asst.

Archaeological Survey of India.

Photo-Lithographed at the Survey of India Offices, Calcutta, March 18[illegible]

1. DETAIL OF SCREEN WORK ON PLATE XIX.

ELEVATION

SCALE
INCHES 12 9 6 3 0 1 FOOT

2. CAPITAL OF PILLAR.

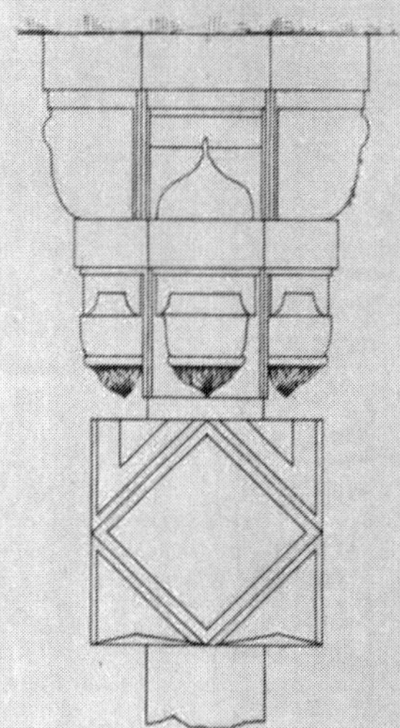

3. CAPITAL.

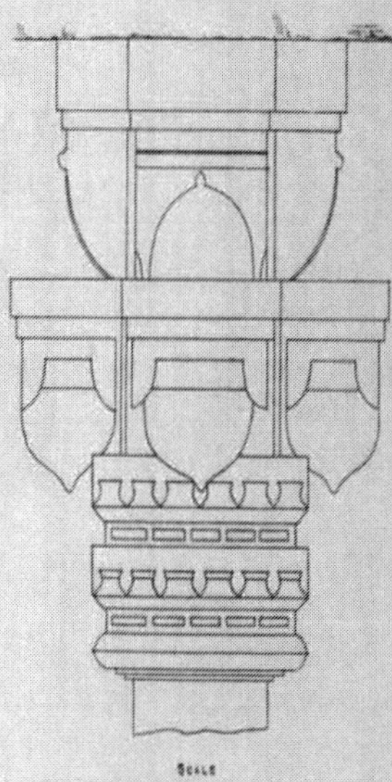

SCALE
INCHES 12 9 6 3 0 1 2 FEET

Archaeological Survey of India.

Photo-lithographed at the Survey of India Offices, Calcutta, March [illegible]

E. W. SMITH,
Architectural Asst.

PLATE XXIII.

JAUNPUR: ATALA MASJID,—EXAMPLES OF PILLARS.

Archaeological Survey of India

Photo-Lithographed at the Survey of India Offices, Calcutta, April [illegible]

E. W. SMITH,
Architectural Asst.

PLATE XXIV.

JAUNPUR: ATALA MASJID.

1. EXTERNAL CORNICE ROUND THE BASE OF THE GREAT DOME.

2. ELEVATION OF BANDS AROUND SPRINGING OF SMALL DOMES.

Scale. Inches. 12 9 6 3 — 1 — 2 Feet.

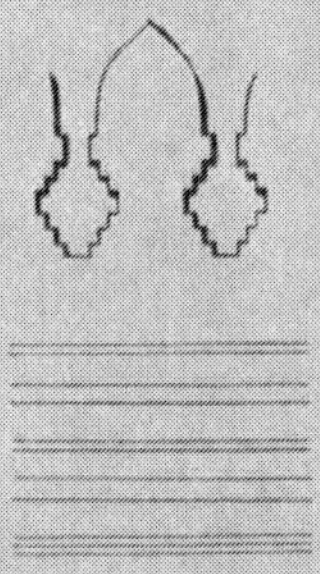

Scale. Inches. 12 6 — 1 — 2 — 3 Feet.

3. BAND AROUND UPPER PORTION OF CENTRAL BAY ON WEST EXTERIOR ELEVATION.

Archaeological Survey of India.

Photo-Lithographed at the Survey of India Offices, Calcutta, April [illegible]

E. W. SMITH,
Architectural Asst.

PLATE XXV

Photo-etching

Survey of India Offices, Calcutta, February 188[illegible]

JAUNPÚR THE JHANJHRI MASJID

PLATE XXV

JAUNPŪR. FRONT OF LĀL DARWĀZA MASJID.

JAUNPUR. INTERIOR OF LĀL DARWĀZA MASJID

PLATE XXVIII.

JAUNPUR: LÂL DARWÂZA MASJID,—GROUND PLAN.

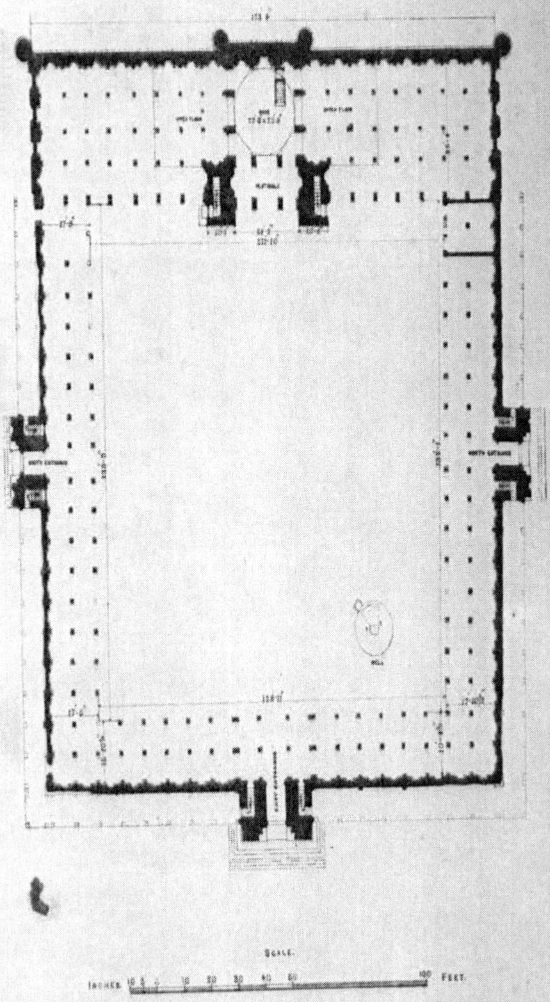

Archaeological Survey of India.

Photo-Lithographed at the Survey of India Offices, Calcutta, July 18[illegible]

EDMD W. SMITH,
Architectural Asst.

JAUNPUR: LAL DARWAZA. PLATE XXIX

1. FRONT OF THE MASJID.

2. SOUTH ELEVATION OF THE EXTENSION.

Archaeological Survey of India.

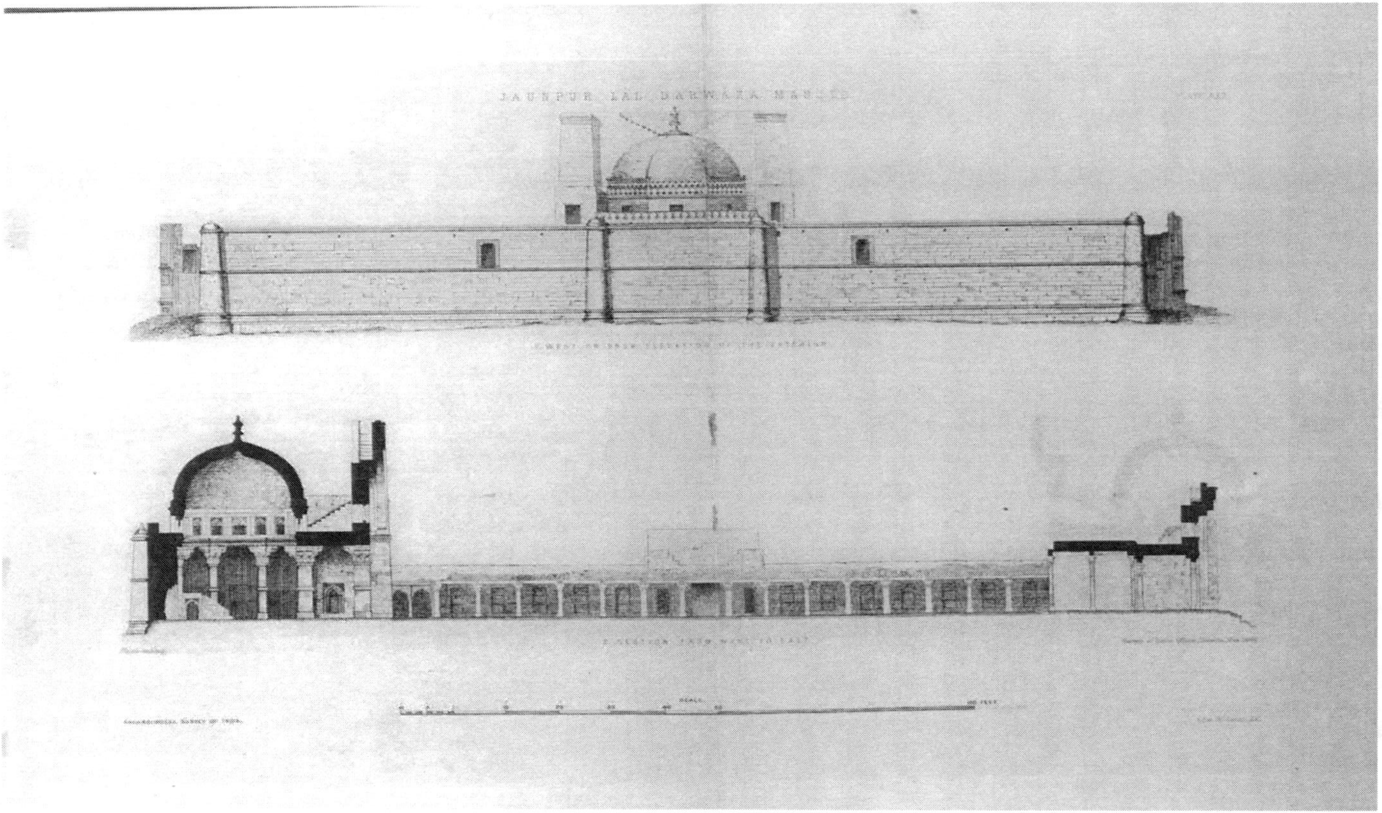
JAUNPUR LAL DARWAZA MASJID

1. SECTION OF ZANANA GALLERY.

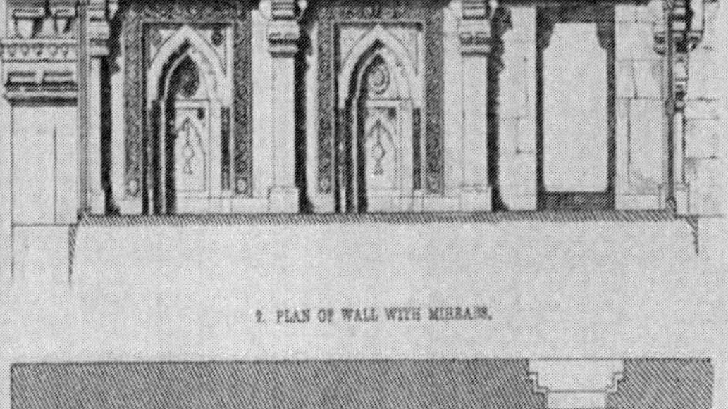

3. SECTION OF MIHRAB.

2. PLAN OF WALL WITH MIHRABS.

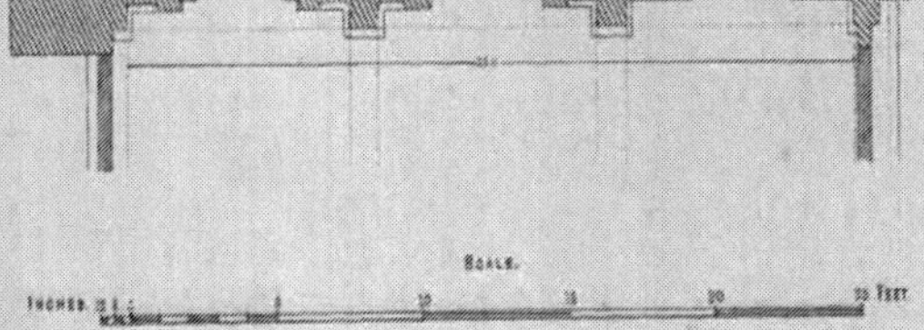

SCALE.

INCHES 12 6 0 5 10 15 20 25 FEET

4. PILASTER OF MIHRAB.

5. DETAIL OF ORNAMENT.

THE NORTH ENTRANCE.

SCALE.

INCHES. 12 6 0 1 2 3 4 5 10 15 20 FEET.

Archaeological Survey of India

Photo-Lithographed at the Survey of India Offices, Calcutta, March [illegible]

EDMD. W. SMITH

Archaeological Asst.

JAUNPUR: LÁL DARWÁZA MASJID. PLATE XXXIII

East or Principal Gateway.

Scale.

Inches 12 6 0 1 2 3 4 5 10 15 20 25 Feet.

Archaeological Survey of India.

Photo-Lithographed at the Survey of India Offices, Calcutta, October [illegible]

EDMD. W. SMITH,
Archaeological Asst.

JAUNPUR: LAL DARWAZA MASJID.

PLATE XXXIV.

1. PRINCIPAL MIHRAB.

2. SECTION.

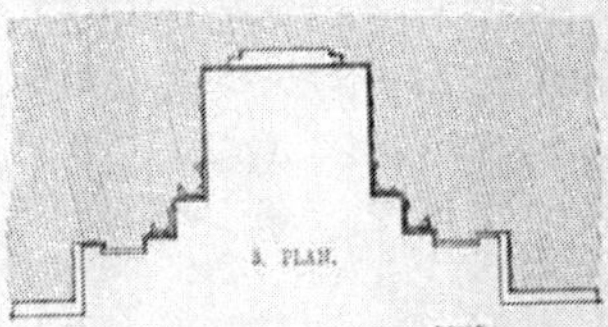

3. PLAN.

SCALE

INCHES 12 6 0 1 2 3 4 5 10 15 FEET

4. A BAY OF THE CLOISTER WALLS.

5. SECTION ACROSS THE CLOISTERS OF THE COURT.

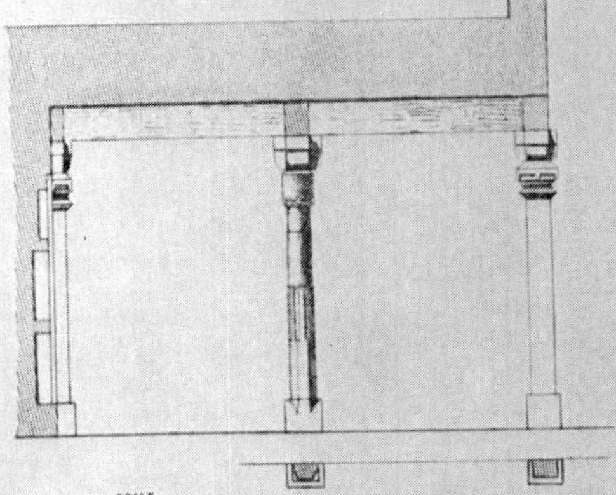

SCALE

INCHES 12 6 0 1 2 3 4 5 10 15 20 FEET

PHOTOZINCOGRAPHED AT THE SURVEY OF INDIA OFFICES, CALCUTTA, APRIL

PLATE XXXV

JAUNPUR LĀL DARWĀZA MASJID

ARCHAEOLOGICAL SURVEY OF INDIA

Edm. W. Smith, del.

MIHRABS ALONG THE INNER WALL

JAUNPUR: LAL DARWAZA MASJID.

PLATE XXXVI.

Panels over the Niches in the West Wall.

Archæological Survey of India.

Photo-Lithographed at the Survey of India Offices, Calcutta, November [illegible].

EDMD. W. SMITH,
Archæological Surveyor.

JAUNPUR LÀL DARWÀZA MASJID

PLATE [illegible]

PLATE XXXVIII.

JAUNPUR: LÂL DARWÂZA MASJID.

WALL PANEL OVER THE PRINCIPAL MIHRÂB.

SCALE.

INCHES. 12 9 6 3 0 1 2 FEET.

Archaeological Survey of India.

Photo-Lithographed at the Survey of India Offices, Calcutta, November [illegible]

EDMD. W. SMITH,
Archaeological Asst.

JAUNPUR: LÂL DARWÂZA MASJID.

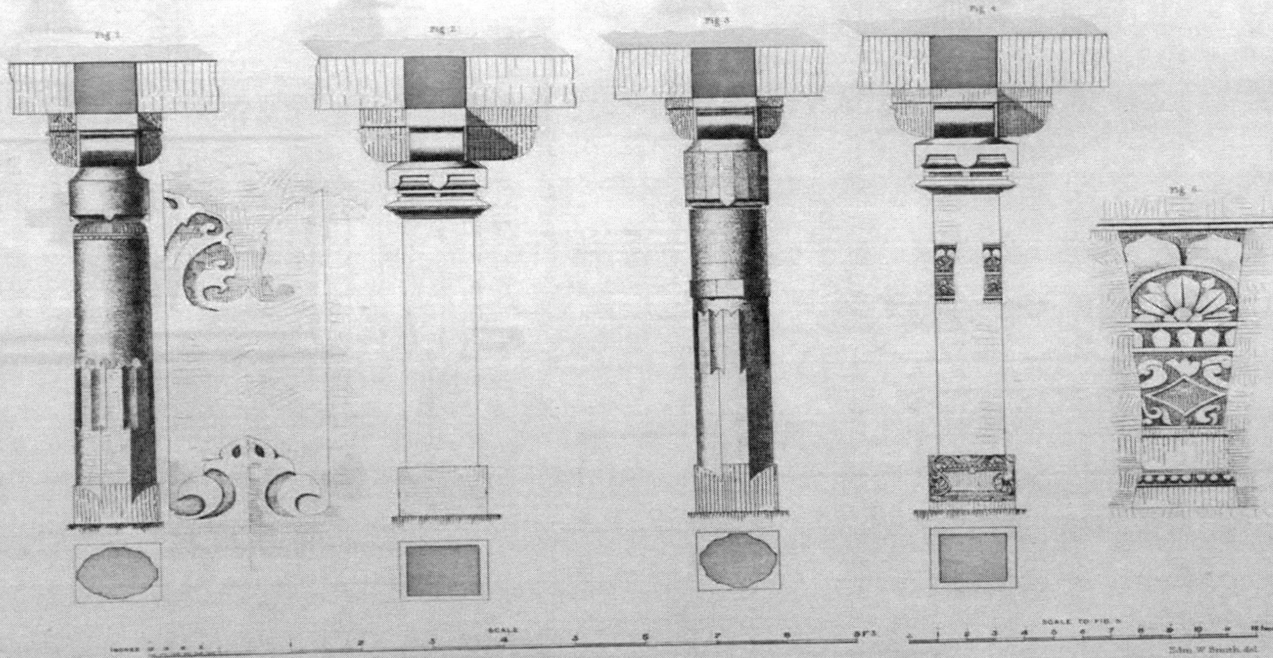

Edm. W. Smith. del.

ARCHAEOLOGICAL SURVEY OF INDIA.

EXAMPLES OF PILLARS IN THE CLOISTERS.

Survey of India Offices, Calcutta, October 1898.

JAUNPUR: LÂL DARWÂZA MASJID. PLATE XL.

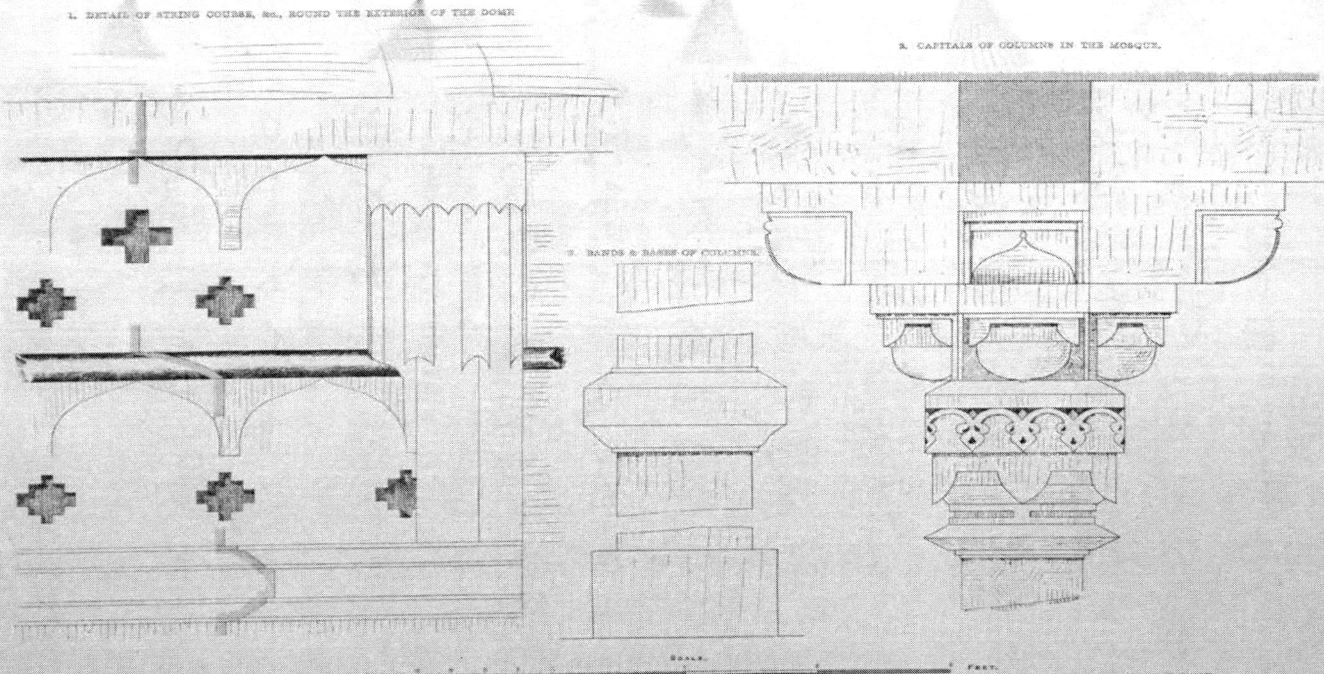

JAUNPUR: MASON'S MARKS,—(1) FROM THE ATÁLA MASJID.

(2) FROM THE LÁL DARWÁZA MASJID.

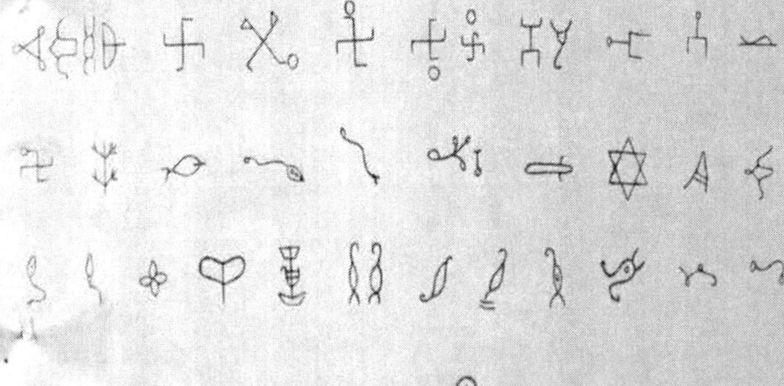

JAUNPUR: MASON'S MARKS,—(3) FROM THE JAMI' MASJID. PLATE XLII.

PLATE XIII

JAUNPUR JĀMĪ MASJID, FAÇADE

JAUNPUR. JĀMĪ MASJID, NORTH EXTERIOR SHOWING THE ARCADE

PLATE XIX

JAUNPUR. JAMI MASJID, SOUTH-WEST EXTERIOR

JAUNPUR: JAMI MASJID,—PLAN OF BASEMENT. PLATE XLVI.

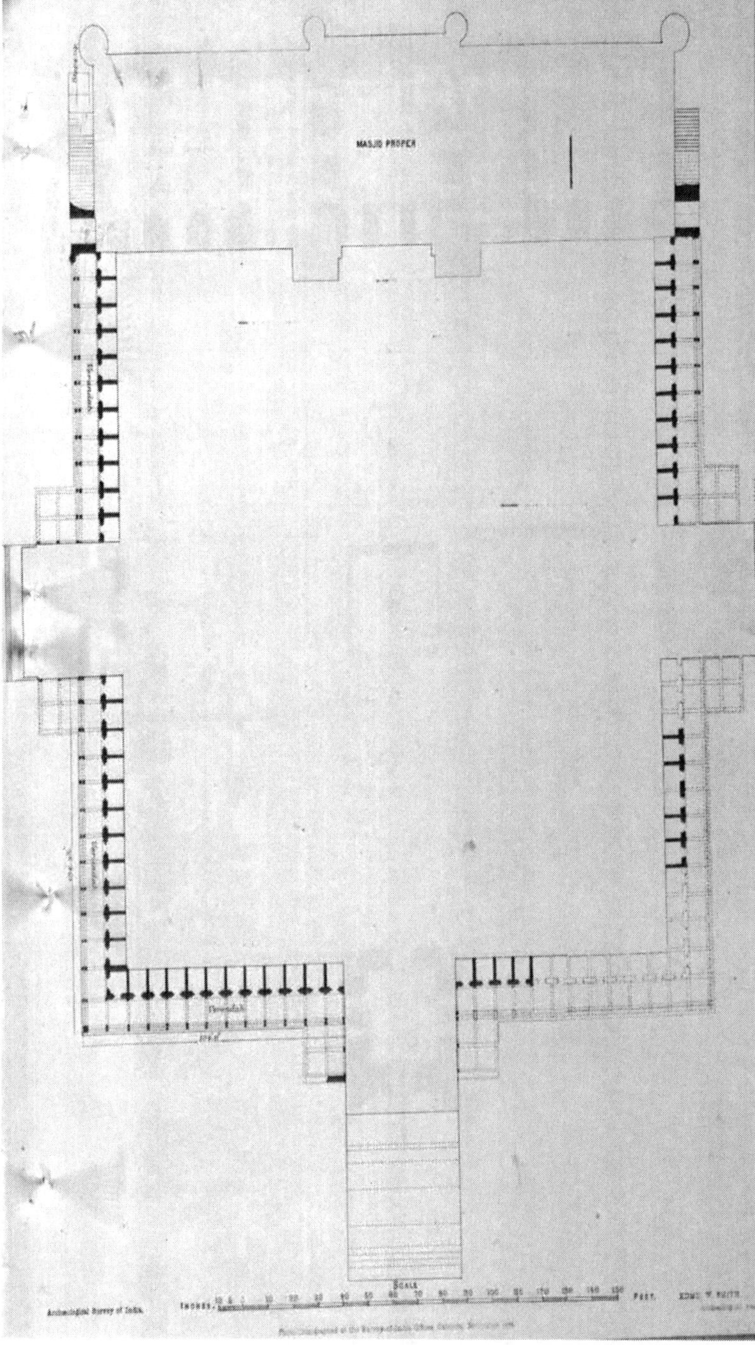

Archaeological Survey of India.

EDMD. W. SMITH.

JAUNPUR: JÂMI' MASJID,—GROUND PLAN. PLATE XLVII.

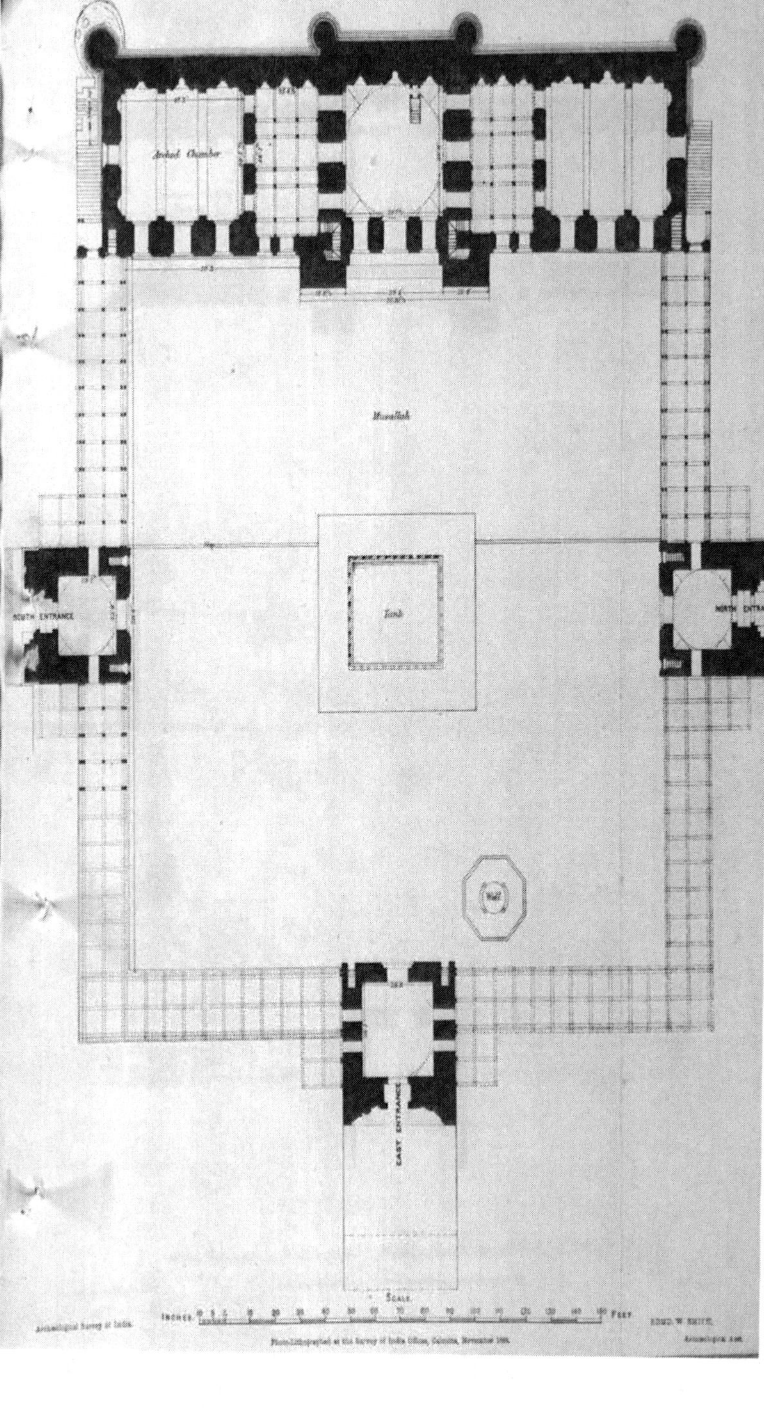

Archaeological Survey of India. EDMD. W. SMITH, Archaeological Asst.

Photo-Lithographed at the Survey of India Offices, Calcutta, November

JAUNPUR: JĀMĪ MASJID,—UPPER PLAN. PLATE XLVIII.

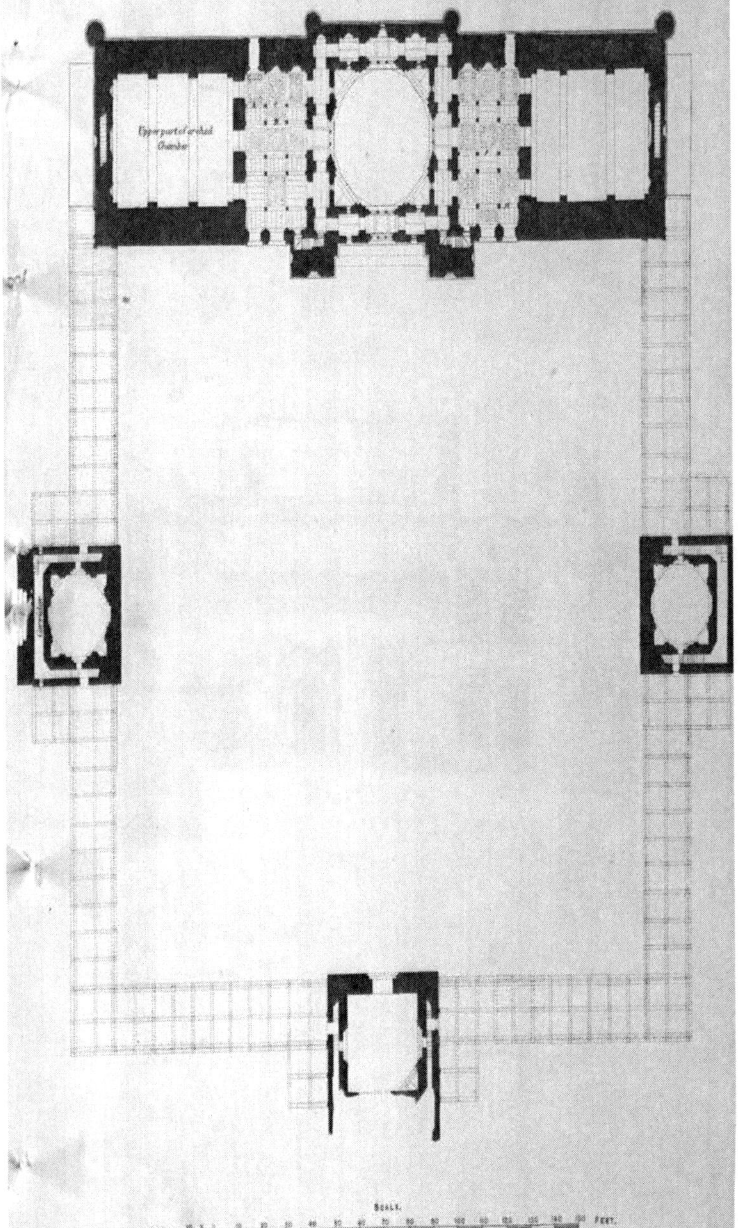

Archæological Survey of India.

Photo-Lithographed at the Survey of India Offices, Calcutta, November

EDMD. W. SMITH, Archæological Surv.

JAUNPUR JÁMI MASJID

FAÇADE AND SECTION OF CORRIDORS

PLATE L.

JAUNPUR: JĀMI' MASJID.

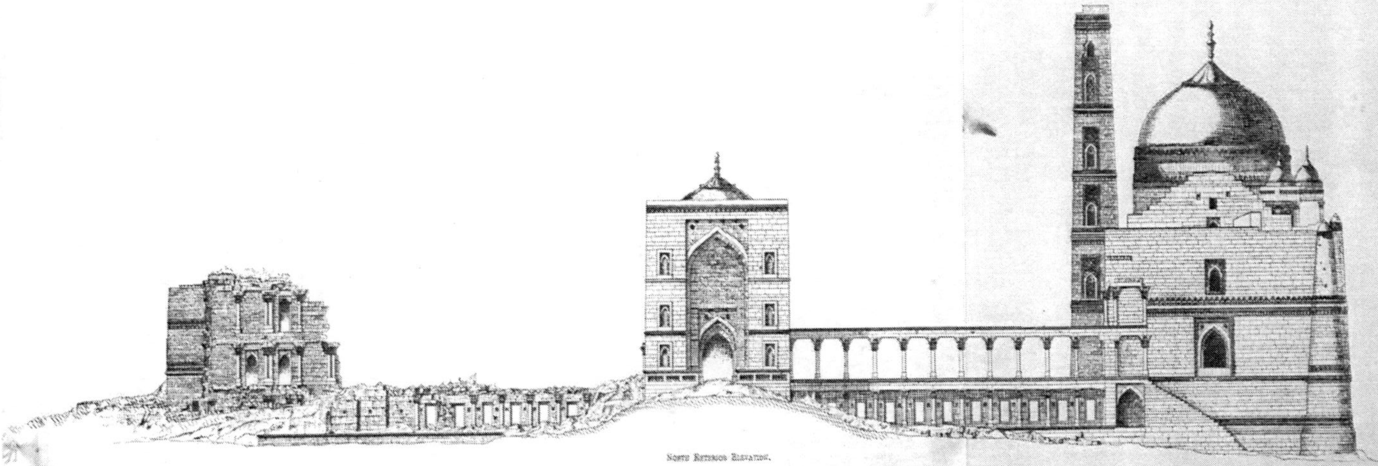

NORTH EXTERIOR ELEVATION.

SCALE

FEET

JAUNPUR JAMI MASJID

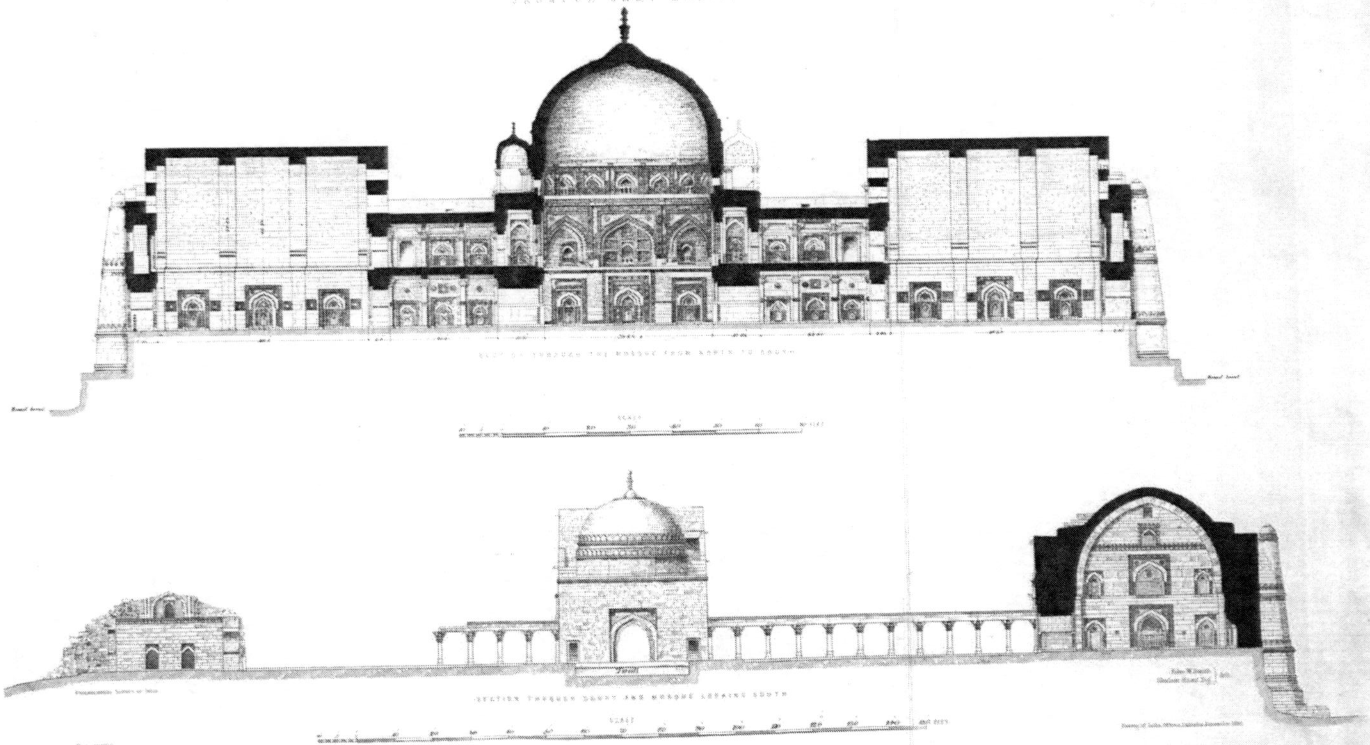

JAUNPUR. JÂMI' MASJID.

PLATE LII.

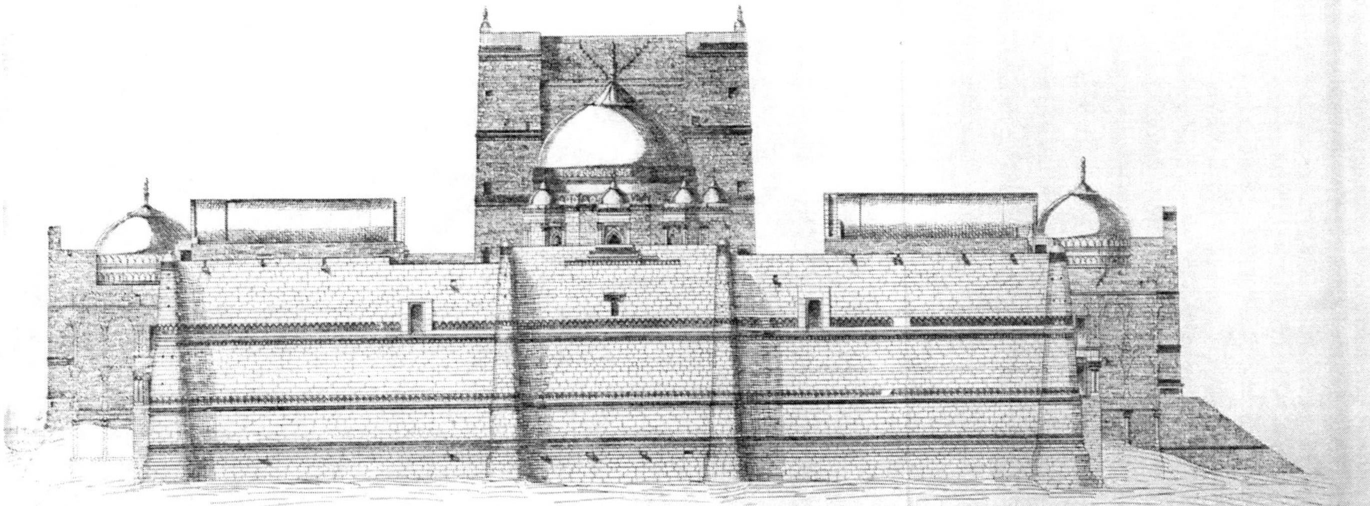

WEST EXTERIOR ELEVATION.

SCALE

0 10 20 30 40 50 60 70 80 90 100 110 120 130 140 150 160 170 FEET.

JAUNPUR: JÂMÍ MASJID. PLATE LIII.

Central Entrance to the Mosque.

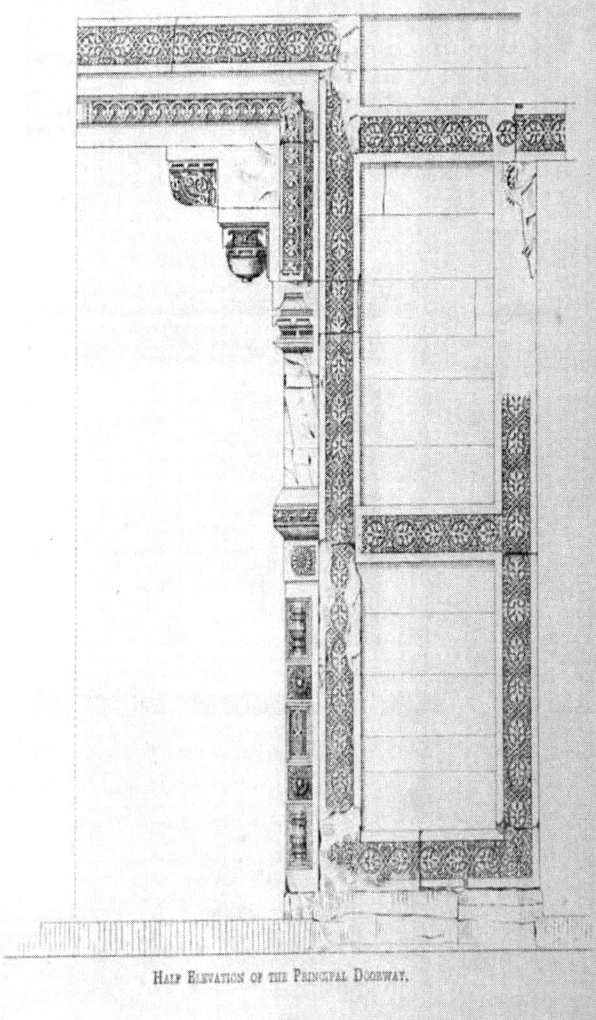

Half Elevation of the Principal Doorway.

Scale.

Inches ... Feet.

Archæological Survey of India.

Photo-Lithographed at the Survey of India Offices, Calcutta, November

JAUNPUR: JÂMI' MASJID. PLATE LIV.

PLATE LV.

JAUNPUR: JÁMÍ MASJID.

SOFFIT OF PRINCIPAL DOORWAY.

SCALE

INCHES 12 9 6 3 0 1 2 3 4 FEET

Photo-Zincographed at the Survey of India Offices, Calcutta, December [illegible]

Archaeological Survey of India.

EDMD. W. SMITH

FAIZ-AD-DIN, [illegible]

LOWEST PANEL IN SOUTH PIER OF THE PROPYLON.

Archaeological Survey of India.

Photo-Lithographed at the Survey of India Offices, Calcutta, November

EDMD. W. SMITH, K. A. BISWAS } del.

PLATE LVII.

JAUNPUR: JÂMÎ' MASJID.

Panels on the North Face of the South Pier of the Propylon.

1. In Second Storey.   2. In Third Storey.   3. In Fourth Storey.

Scale.

Inches. 12 ... 10 ... 15 ... 20 Feet.

Fazl-ad-dîn, del.

Edmd. W. Smith, Archaeological Asst.

Photo-Lithographed at the Survey of India Offices, Calcutta, November [illegible]

Archaeological Survey of India.

1. TOP STOREY OF SOUTH PIER OF PROPYLON,—NORTH FACE.

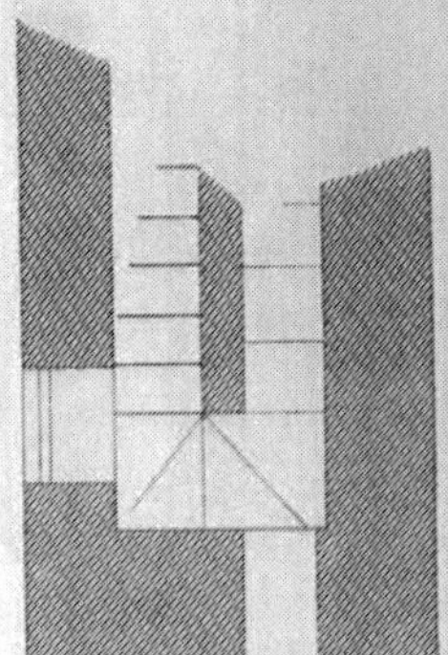

2. PLAN.

SCALE

[illegible] 1 2 3 4 5 10 15 20 FEET.

Archaeological Survey of India. Photo-lithographed at the Survey of India Offices, Calcutta, February [illegible]. EDMD. W. SMITH, Archaeological Surv.

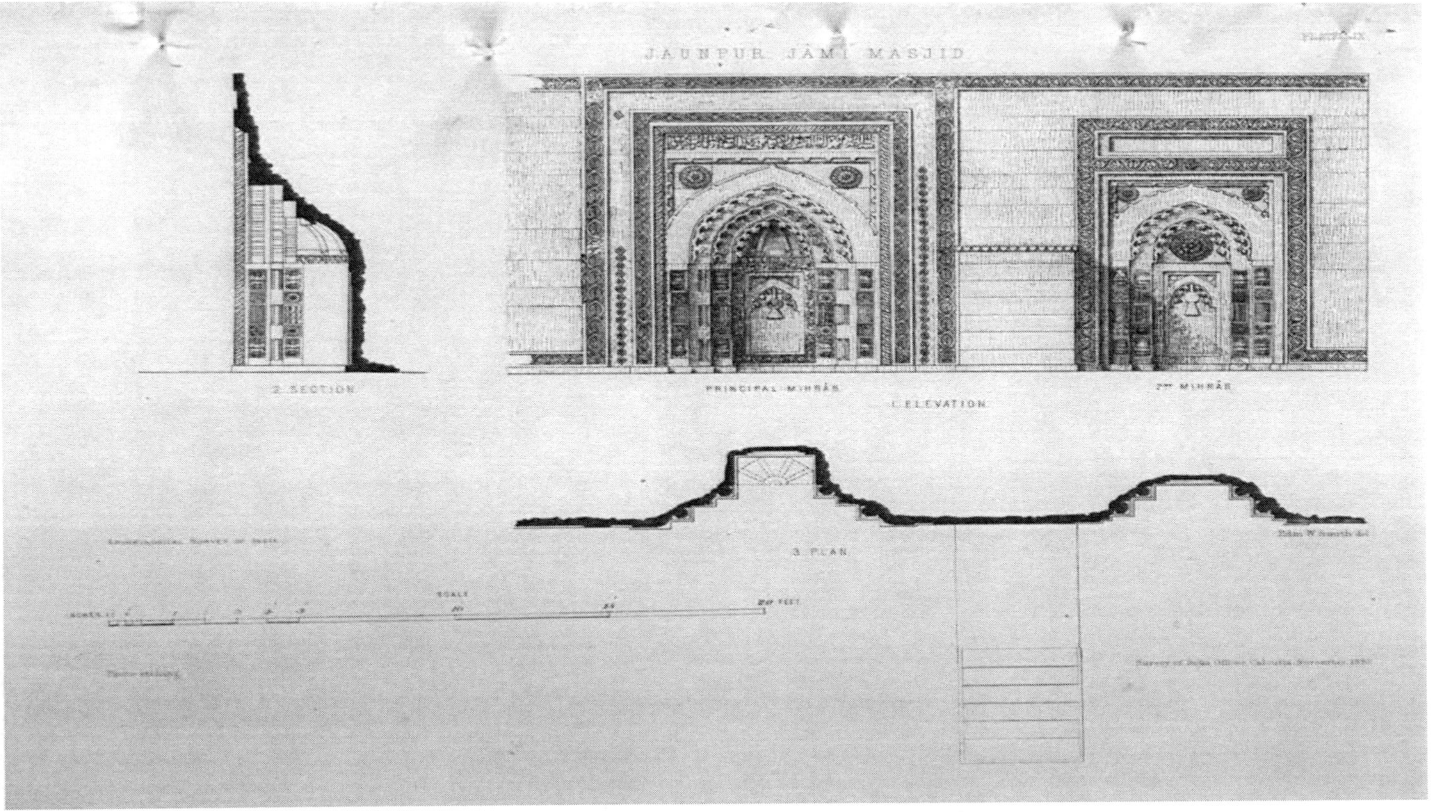
JAUNPUR JĀMI MASJID
2. SECTION
PRINCIPAL MIHRĀB
2ND MIHRĀB
1. ELEVATION
3. PLAN
SCALE
20 FEET

JAUNPUR: JÀMÍ' MASJID.

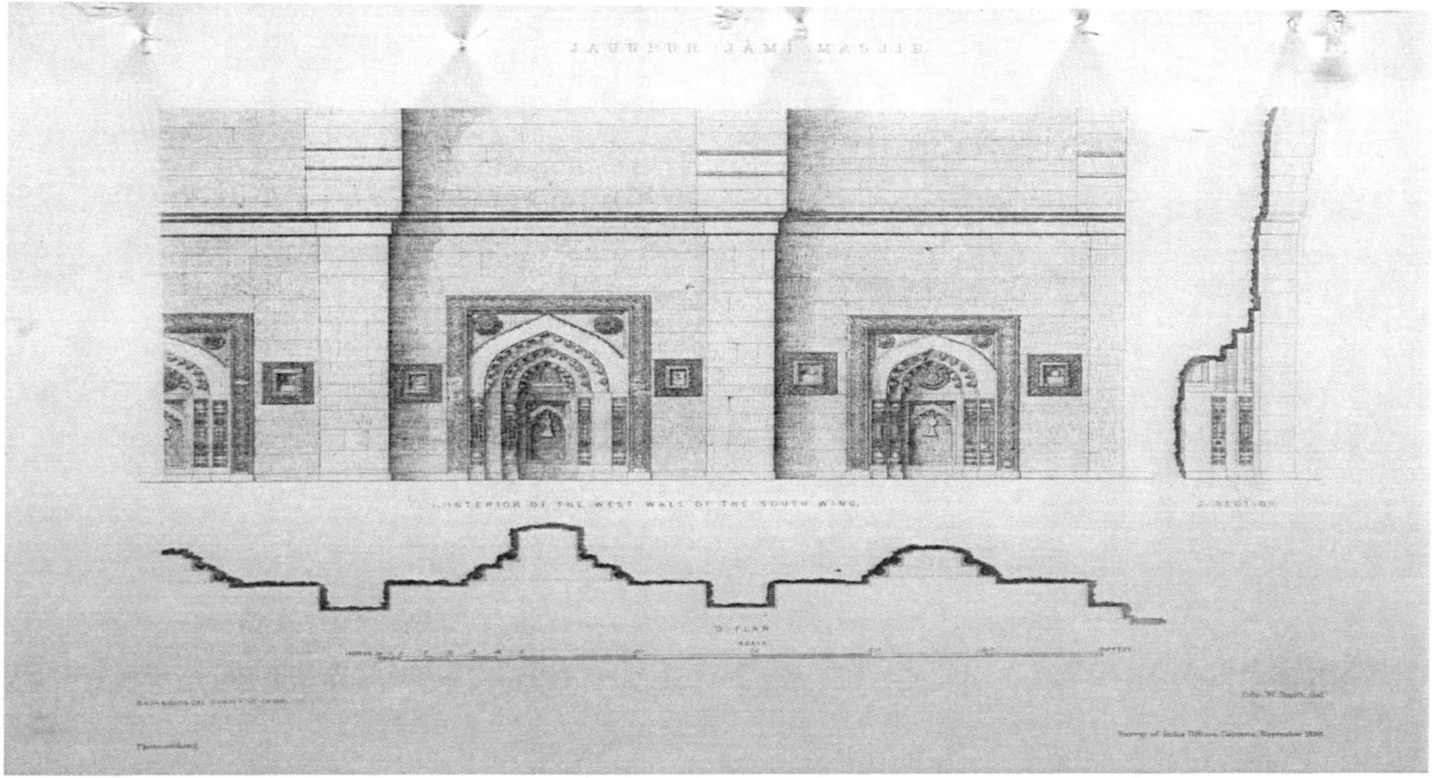
JAUNPUR JĀMI MASJID
1. INTERIOR OF THE WEST WALL OF THE SOUTH WING.
2. SECTION
3. PLAN

PLATE LXII.

JAUNPUR: JÂMI' MASJID.

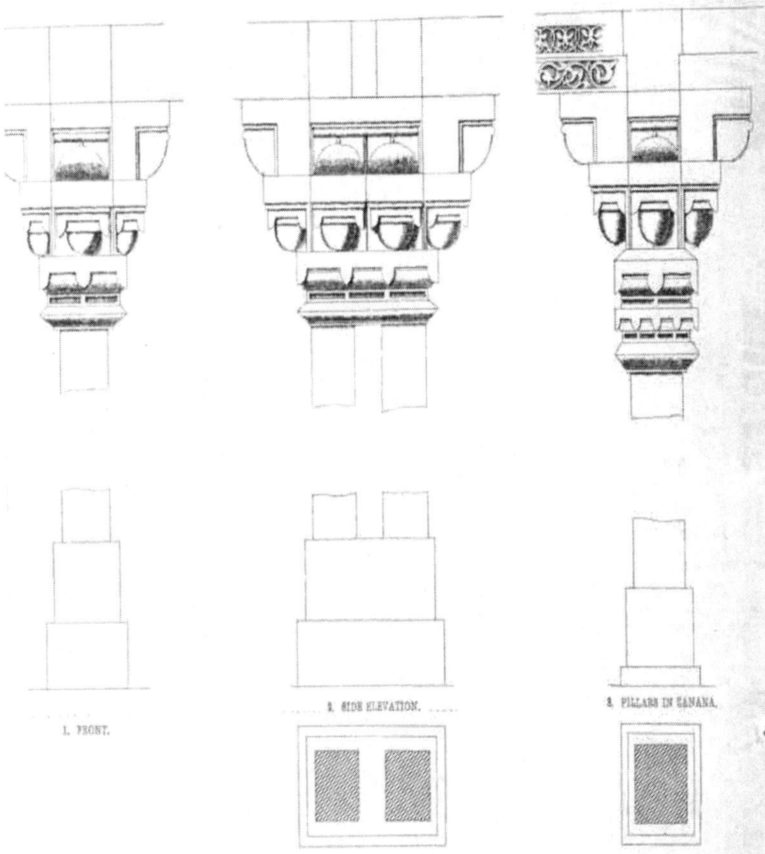

1. FRONT.

2. SIDE ELEVATION.

3. PILLARS IN ZANANA.

DETAILS OF PILLARS.

SCALE

INCHES 12 9 6 3 0 1 2 3 4 5 6 7 8 FEET.

Photo-lithographed at the Survey of India Offices, Calcutta, April 188[illegible]

EDMD. W. SMITH,
Asst. Archl. Archaeological Surveyor,
North West Provinces and Oudh Circle.

PLATE LXIII
JAUNPUR JAMI MASJID
1. ELEVATION
2. SECTION
3. PLAN
SCALE
MIHRAB IN SOUTH ZANANA GALLERY

JAUNPUR JĀMI MASJID

MIHRĀB IN NORTH ZANĀNA GALLERY

JAUNPUR, JĀMĪ MASJID

1. PANEL A IN THE ROOF OF THE ZANĀNA GALLERY.

Archaeological Survey of India.

SCALE

INCHES 12 9 6 3 0 — 1 — 2 — 3 — 4 — 5 FEET

2. PANEL B IN THE ROOF OF THE ZANĀNA GALLERY.

JAUNPUR. JÁMI MASJID.

Archæological Survey of India.

SCALE

PANEL G IN THE ROOF OF THE SOUTH ZANÁNA GALLERY.

JAUNPŪR JĀMĪ MASJID

1 CEILING PANEL I IN NORTH ZANĀNA GALLERY

Archaeological Survey of India

2 CEILING PANEL II IN NORTH ZANĀNA GALLERY

SCALE

10 FEET

JAUNPUR: JÂMI' MASJID.

1. PANEL ON N. SIDE OF CENTRAL MIHRAB IN SOUTH WING.

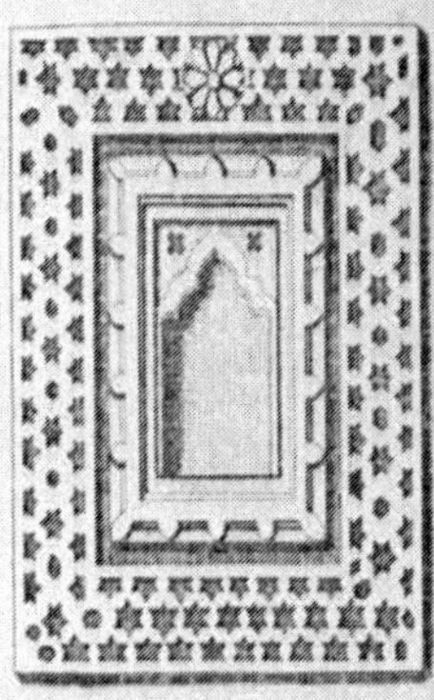

2. PANEL ON N. SIDE OF CENTRAL MIHRAB IN THE NORTH WING.

3. TOP OF THE TURRETS.

SCALE TO FIGS. 1 & 2

INCHES 12 9 6 3 0 1 2 FEET

4. DETAIL OF UPPER STRING-COURSE.

SCALE TO FIGS. 3 & 4

INCHES 12 9 6 3 0 1 2 3 4 5 6 7 FEET

Photolithographed at the Survey of India Offices, Calcutta, May 18[illegible]

EDMD. W. SMITH,
Architectural Asst.

Archaeological Survey of India.

PLATE LXIX.

JAUNPUR: JÂMIʿ MASJID.

1. DETAIL OF LOWER STRING-COURSE ON THE WEST FAÇADE.

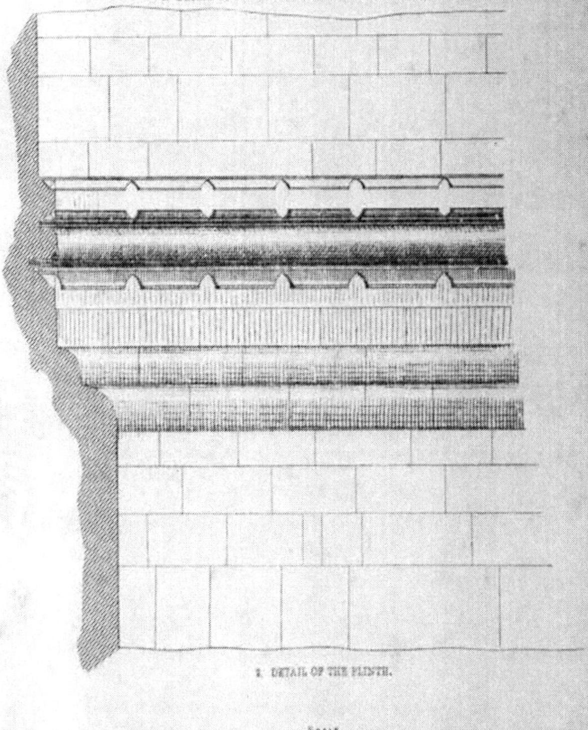

2. DETAIL OF THE PLINTH.

SCALE

INCHES 12 9 6 3 0 1 2 3 4 5 6 7 FEET

Archæological Survey of India.

Photo-lithographed at the Survey of India Offices, Calcutta, May [illegible]

EDMD. W. SMITH.

Architectural Surv.

JAUNPUR: JÂMI' MASJID. PLATE LXX.

DETAIL OF LOWER FRIEZE ROUND GREAT DOME.

SCALE

FEET

Archaeological Survey of India. Photo-lithographed at the Survey of India Offices, Calcutta, February

EDMD. W. SMITH,
Archaeological

2. DETAIL OF FRIEZE ROUND THE KIOSKS AT THE ANGLES OF THE GREAT DOME.

1. DETAIL OF UPPER FRIEZE ROUND EXTERIOR OF THE GREAT DOME.

Archæological Survey of India. Photo-lithographed at the Survey of India Offices, Calcutta, February

1. SOUTH ENTRANCE GATEWAY.

2. SECTION.

3. HALF PLAN.

Archaeological Survey of India.

Photo-lithographed at the Survey of India Offices, Calcutta, February 18[illegible].

EDMD. W. SMITH,
Archaeological Surveyor.

JAUNPUR: JÂMI' MASJID. PLATE LXXIII.

1. SECTION OF NORTH ENTRANCE GATE.

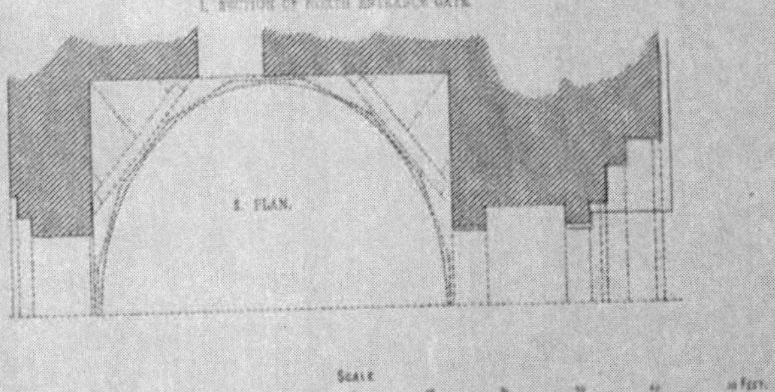

Archaeological Survey of India.

Photolithographed at the Survey of India Offices, Calcutta, February

EDMD. W. SMITH

SAHET-MAHET INSCRIPTION OF VIDYÂDHARA: SAMVAT 1176.

Scale 1-3rd of original.